KT-441-534

Raising achievement: a guide to successful strategies

Paul Martinez

Published by FEDA

Feedback and orders should be sent to FEDA publications
Citadel Place, Tinworth Street, London SE11 5EF
Tel: 020 7840 5302/4 Fax: 020 7840 5401
FEDA on the Internet – www.feda.ac.uk

Registered with the Charity Commissioners

Editors: Angela Dewsbury and Jackie Mace
Designers: Jason Billin, Joel Quartey and Dave Shaw
Printed by: Copyprint Ltd, London

ISBN 1 85338 535 2

© 2000 FEDA

FEDA's RQA programme
FEDA's Raising Quality and Achievement (RQA) programme
is a three-year initiative, funded by the DfEE, to support
colleges in their drive to improve students' achievement
and the quality of provision. The programme offers:

- Quality information and advice service
- Quality improvement team
- Benchmarking and information
- Development projects
- Leadership and governance
- Best practice.

The programme is run in collaboration with the
Association of Colleges (AoC) and operates in close
liaison with the FEFC's Quality Improvement Unit.

Contents

Foreword
Baroness Blackstone

Raising levels of participation, achievement and retention, and promoting higher standards of teaching are the most critical challenges facing the further education (FE) sector.

The Government believes that further education has a major role to play in widening participation, increasing opportunity and developing a knowledge-based economy for the 21st century. To achieve these objectives, colleges need to build on the progress already made to raise standards and improve achievement.

The Standards Fund initiative, launched by this Government, is providing the sector with targeted funding to raise standards and quality of provision. The work reported in this guide shows how the Standards Fund is being used to support college-based initiatives. The guide also provides practical information based on over 20 case studies on the activity of teachers, curriculum managers and student support staff.

The messages in this guide are relevant to all FE institutions. Those whose work and initiatives are described here have developed successful techniques to raise achievement. I am sure that you and your college will find the techniques equally useful.

Baroness Blackstone
Minister of State for Education

Acknowledgements

This report is based on the hard work of teachers and managers in the following colleges and adult education services. Particular thanks are due to:

Trevor Cotterill, Arnold & Carlton College, Nottingham (now part of New College Nottingham)
Steve Mohan, Barking College
Fintan Donohue, Barnfield College
Debbie Vaughan, Barnsley College
Celia Beizsley, Basford Hall College (now part of New College Nottingham)
Julie Chapman, Bridgend College
Sumitar Young, Bridgwater College
Julian Clissold, Burnley College
Cath Hurst, Bury College
Hugh Joslin, Canterbury College
Frank McCann, Carmel College, Merseyside
Janet Pittaway, Dewsbury College
Phil Butler, East Birmingham College (now part of City College Birmingham)
Allan Rowe, Epping Forest College
Jenny Kirk, Gloucestershire Adult and Community Education and Training (ACET)
Andy Hodgson, Great Yarmouth College of Further Education
Kevin Conway, Greenhead College
Paul Devall, Harrogate College
Michael Bretherick, Hartlepool College of Further Education
Chris Woodrow, Huddersfield New College
Ian Rothery, Lewes Tertiary College
Ann Lees, Liverpool Community College
Jackie Doodson, Llandrillo College
Ian Wilson, Long Road Sixth Form College
Helen Nicholson, Lowestoft College

Maggie Chattaway, Luton Sixth Form College
Charles Anderson, North Warwickshire and Hinckley College
Ros Tansley-Thomas, Norwich City College
Ruth Durbridge, Oxford College
Christine Sullivan, Palmer's College
Stephanie Quant, Reading College and School of Arts and Design
Peter Bignold, Regent College, Leicester
Ann Risman, Richmond Adult and Community College
Elaine Smith, Runshaw College, Lancashire
Suzie Knight, The Solihull College
Janis Evans, Solihull Sixth Form College
Sue Forrest, South Birmingham College
Tony Pitcher, South East Essex College
Lesley Hughes, South Nottingham College
Peter Brook, Sparsholt College
Marilyn Watsham, Suffolk College
Martyn Park, Sutton Coldfield College
Tricia Burton, Telford College of Arts and Technology
Eddie Playfair, Tower Hamlets College
Rachel Davis, Uxbridge College
Lyn Beverley, Walsall College of Arts and Technology
Sue Warman, West Herts College
Liz Whittome, West Kent College
Kevin Watson, Winstanley College, Wigan
Shelagh Ferguson, Wirral Metropolitan College
Cliff Hall, Wulfrun College (now part of Wolverhampton College)
John Cartmell, Yale College, Wrexham

1 | Context and objectives

We do not know enough about what works in further education and why. The truth of this sweeping statement can be demonstrated quite easily. The British Educational Index contains details of all books, articles and many research dissertations published in Britain in the field of education. If you search on 'teaching' and similar terms, you will generate thousands of entries. If you search on 'teaching' and 'effectiveness' (or 'teaching' and 'achievement'), there are a few hundred entries. If you restrict the search on the paired terms to further or tertiary education, there are almost no entries.

This guide is the result of some two years' work with a wide variety of colleges and a few adult education services. It has been published to coincide with a large number of initiatives designed to improve achievement within the broad framework of the further education Standards Fund (in England).

The Standards Fund is designed to improve quality and raise achievement through a number of strategies including:

- Financial support to remedy weaknesses in colleges that are deemed to be causing concern
- Post-inspection support to develop and deliver college action plans to address issues raised by inspections
- Leadership training and continuing professional development (CPD)
- Funding to Beacon and accredited colleges to enable them to disseminate good practice
- A Raising Quality and Achievement programme delivered by FEDA with the Association of Colleges (AoC).

The Standards Fund complements other initiatives with similar objectives:

- Accredited college status
- National standards for teaching in further education
- The FEFC's Inclusive Learning initiative
- The requirement to set and report progress towards targets for retention and achievement.

Similar objectives are being pursued by government, funding and inspection agencies in Wales, Scotland and Northern Ireland.

Within this context, the purposes of this guide are to:

- Review the experience of a number of colleges that have been successful in raising achievement
- Make their experience available in an accessible form
- Provide a synthesis and overview
- Suggest further reading
- Complement the earlier guide, *Improving student retention* (Martinez, 1997), and in so doing:
  - Support you and your college in the development of your own strategies to raise achievement
  - Encourage the spread of action research and evidence-based approaches to curriculum design and teaching.

There is substantial evidence from FEDA's research (FEDA, 1998) that, for GNVQs, issues around achievement are closely linked to those around retention. Many of the colleges whose work is reviewed here make little or no distinction in their improvement strategies between the two. Accordingly, while the focus of this guide remains achievement, the term has been construed broadly and references will be made to retention strategies and (briefly) to the work of the colleges synthesised in *Improving student retention* (Martinez, 1997).

Focus

Strategies for raising achievement for younger and older, academic and vocational students will be reviewed. However, the extent to which each group is covered varies between chapters, reflecting the uneven nature of developments within the sector. Chapters 3 and 5 on student motivation and tutoring, respectively, tend to focus more on younger, full-time students. Chapter 8 explores a number of issues around achievement that are particular to adult, mainly part-time students. The chapter on value added (Chapter 4) gives slightly more prominence to applications in an academic (A-level) context but the developments in vocational areas are also explored in some detail.

The case studies used throughout the report attempt to strike a balance between different levels, programme areas, types of institutions, types of students and academic and vocational subjects. They are presented in a common format: problems, applied strategies and outcomes.

Method

The research on which this guide is based was qualitative in nature. Two national surveys were carried out to identify colleges that had implemented successful strategies to improve achievement, retention or both. The surveys were supplemented by informal networking, contacts with college managers and researchers, and the scrutiny of published performance data.

Colleges that had improved achievement and were willing to share their experiences with others were invited to present their strategies at a number of conferences and seminars held between autumn 1997 and summer 1999. This guide represents a synthesis of their work.

Structure

Research evidence suggests that strategies that affect student experience directly are most likely to raise achievement. The guide has, accordingly, been organised in three main sections:

- Chapters 3–5 introduce some of the most widely implemented strategies used to:
  - Improve student motivation
  - Develop value added approaches
  - Extend and refine arrangements for tutoring.

- Chapters 6–9 review strategies related to teaching, learning and the curriculum, namely:
  - Teaching and pedagogy
  - Curriculum design, structure and strategy
  - Adult achievement and issues around the assessment of adult learning
  - Support for achievement: processes that mediate student learning including advice and guidance, recruitment and selection, induction and settling in.

- Chapters 10–11 examine issues around motivating staff, processes of managing and implementing change, management at different levels and possible combinations of top-down and bottom-up approaches.

Each chapter includes a summary of key points and these are brought together in the final chapter. Appendix 1 provides a brief summary of the scope and outcomes of the strategies pursued in the different institutions.

However, before exploring any of these issues the next chapter will explain (and perhaps justify) the approach used, clarify terms and create a framework for reviewing and analysing this experience. It will do so by challenging some apparently widely held beliefs about student achievement.

2

Beliefs about student achievement

Myths, assumptions, and other untested beliefs will usually rush in to fill a vacuum associated with a lack of knowledge and research. Student achievement is no exception. It may well be that such beliefs are particularly prevalent in relation to student achievement given that the issue is:

- Highly charged emotionally – teachers' feelings of self-worth are closely linked with the success of their students
- Under intense scrutiny – from managers, parents, inspectors, politicians and other stakeholders
- Complicated and difficult – and hence not amenable to simplistic and mechanistic solutions.

Myths about achievement

Expressed in their most robust form, myths and untested beliefs about achievement would include the views that:

- Widening participation is not compatible with raising achievement
- Raising achievement is not compatible with improving retention
- Demography is destiny
- 'My subject is too difficult'
- 'It's all out of our hands'
- We can only progress with a charismatic principal
- We can only progress with charismatic teachers
- There are 10 golden rules to improve achievement.

The rest of this chapter discusses and challenges each of these beliefs in turn.

Widening participation is not compatible with raising achievement

The view that widening participation is not compatible with raising achievement is frequently articulated in the pages of *The Times Educational Supplement*. It comes from the apparently commonsense assumption that the more that excluded and marginal groups take up further education opportunities, the less likely they are to complete their courses and achieve qualifications.

This argument can be challenged on empirical and logical grounds. Empirically, many of the successful strategies reviewed here have been developed with students who have a history of poor prior attainment, educational or social disadvantage. Similar accounts of success with non-traditional students can be found in the appendix to the Kennedy Report (Kennedy, 1997) and in the forthcoming FEFC survey on widening participation (FEFC, 2000).

In terms of logic, further education does not discriminate between those achieving a qualification at entry level and those achieving one at level 4 or 5.

Achievement is achievement is achievement. This is the unique characteristic of further education as compared with the school and higher education sectors. Educators in further education start from the proposition that a person can succeed assuming that s/he is appropriately placed and taught on a programme. This does presuppose that colleges have an appropriate curriculum and that student advice and support systems are in place. These, in turn, depend on resources. Subject to the necessary curriculum and resources being available, there is no obvious reason why students recruited from different parts of the community should not achieve their qualification aims (AoC, 1999; Martinez, 1999a).

However, there are some specific issues that relate to the achievement of qualifications by some adult students. These are discussed in Chapter 8.

Raising achievement is not compatible with improving retention

There is a widespread belief that the more we encourage students to stay on their courses, the lower will be the proportion of students who pass their exams. This view is also expressed in reverse: the easiest (or the only) way to increase achievement rates is to get rid of (or not enter) the least able or most marginal students for exams.

As will be seen in this guide, in almost all colleges improvements to achievement go hand in hand with improvements to retention. The evidence presented to a Parliamentary Select Committee in February 1999, moreover, contains a detailed study from Lewisham College, which has widened participation in a very deprived community at the same time as increasing retention, achievement and levels of student satisfaction (House of Commons, 1999).

There is a common thread which runs through strategies relating to student motivation, value added, tutoring, assessment and curriculum redesign: students who are achieving as they go along are more likely to persist and achieve. Success may be one of the keys to retention.

Non-completion of GNVQs (FEDA, 1998) shows that evaluations by withdrawn and partially successful students differ in significant ways from evaluations made by successful students. The implication of the research is that for GNVQs, retention and achievement are closely linked, on the one hand, as are drop-out and only partial success, on the other.

However, there is some anecdotal evidence that in relation to qualifications such as A-levels (at least in their linear version) teachers sometimes feel reluctant to encourage weaker students to stay on, because of fears that the average point scores will be reduced. The current public reporting framework which focuses on passes and grades in relation to entries rather than to enrolments, could be said to exacerbate this tension.

If this is an instance where retention and achievement are opposed, it is likely to be transitory because:

- Many colleges have already adopted modular A-levels and all A-levels will in effect become modular from 2001
- All A-levels contain ongoing coursework and assignments, and students will be creating in their own minds the link between success and staying on
- Formative value added methodologies that are based on predicted achievements are also associated with improvements in retention (see Chapter 4).

Demography is destiny

Closely related to the belief that widening participation is inversely related to raising achievement is the view that the demographic profile of the student population largely determines student achievement. Again, the available evidence does not support this view.

Figure 1 shows the relationship between two variables: the percentage of students in sixth form colleges from the most disadvantaged and deprived postcodes (as defined by FEFC) and the percentage of students in the same colleges achieving their qualifications aims. In England, this postcode classification will generate increased funding for colleges with the highest percentage of students from the most deprived postcodes. Sixth form colleges have been selected because of the relatively homogeneous nature of their student populations. The correlation coefficient is 0·1. This suggests that there is little relationship between the two variables. By way of contrast, an example of a relatively strong relationship is the correlation coefficient between average GCSE score and A-levels: 0·70. GCSE grades account for some 50% of the weight of the accepted model between GCSE grades and A-level grades (the square of the correlation coefficient). In the case of the relationship between postcodes and achievement, this falls to 1%.

Figure 1. Relationship between achievement rates and percentage of students from deprived areas designated by postcode in sixth form colleges, 1996–97

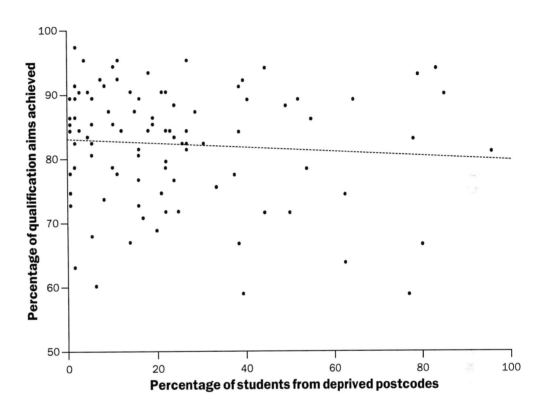

This data needs to be treated with caution. It is based on aggregated data rather than individual student records. Moreover, there is some evidence that deprivation (as measured by postcodes) impacts more strongly on retention than on achievement. There are, thirdly, relatively few sixth form colleges contained in the analysis above. It does, nevertheless, provide some persuasive evidence that achievement and deprivation are not inextricably linked.

This argument is supported by two other sorts of evidence. Firstly, in any college it is almost always possible to find groups of students with similar demographic characteristics but different achievement rates. Against any indicator of educational disadvantage (membership of certain ethnic minority communities, for example), there will almost invariably be a considerable range of achievement rates across (and sometimes even within) colleges.

Secondly, a recent FEDA study has drawn similar conclusions in respect of student part-time work. While excessive part-time work seems to have an adverse effect on student achievement, long hours do not appear to be associated primarily with student hardship or social class (Davies, 1999).

'My subject is too difficult'

There is unequivocal evidence that some A-level subjects, notably the sciences, are more difficult than others (Fitz-Gibbon and Vincent, 1997). There is also substantial anecdotal evidence that some exams set by professional bodies are relatively difficult, either because of outmoded views of standards (high standards require high rates of failure) or because of a continuing commitment to norm referenced assessment (a given percentage of candidates must fail each year).

Such 'truths' acquire mythical status when they are pushed too far. This point can be illustrated by reference to value added and to benchmarking methodologies.

Two of the main value added methods adopted by colleges are the A-level Performance System (ALPS) developed at Greenhead College and the A-level Information System (ALIS) developed by Carole Fitz-Gibbon and currently based at the University of Durham. The ALPS differs from the ALIS in that it:

- Is based exclusively on a college's own data set (rather than national data)
- Treats all A-levels as being of equal difficulty.

As shall be seen in Chapter 4, the ALPS system seems to be as useful as ALIS in terms of providing a methodology for formative assessment and informing pro-fessional and managerial judgements about quality and the curriculum.

In relation to benchmarking, there is substantial anecdotal evidence that the practice of many course teams is relatively underdeveloped. To depict a series of worse-case scenarios (simplified almost to the point of caricature), course teams may benchmark against their own data ('our course has always been difficult'), against largely imaginary data ('well, it has always been difficult in our area') or against real but average national data ('we are just below/at/just above the national average'). The point that will emerge again and again in the case studies that follow is that some of the biggest improvements in achievement rates have occurred when teams set themselves the target of being better than average or have benchmarked themselves against better than average programmes or courses in other colleges.

To return to the original point, some subjects are more difficult than others, but the evidence suggests that even within these constraints of subject difficulty, substantial improvements are possible.

'It's all out of our hands'

All of the myths reviewed so far are echoed in the beliefs that 'teachers cannot make a difference' or 'it is all the fault of somebody else: students, the economy, managers, inspectors etc.'. A slight variation on this theme is that college results would be much better if only all students with poor entry grades were excluded. The evidence points emphatically in the opposite direction. Appendix 1 summ-arises the improvements in achievement and/or retention associated with the strategies discussed in this report.

We can only progress with a charismatic principal

One of the truisms from the literature around managing change is that 'you have got to have support from the top'. By implication, if the support of the principal is not forthcoming, you are stuck!

While some of the strategies reviewed in this report are supported and led by principals and other senior managers, a number are inspired by heads of faculty or department, heads of school or programme area, by course directors and course teams and by individual teachers. The implication is that support from the top is helpful, but that course teams and departments will usually have considerable discretion in the way in which they design, deliver and monitor the curriculum.

We can only progress with charismatic teachers

The view was once put by a (now retired) principal that 'to teach the kids we have got these days, you have to be a superhero'. The rather more widespread version of this belief is that improving student achievement requires some sort of supreme commitment, effort or charismatic personality on the part of teachers.

There are many highly committed, extremely hard-working and charismatic teachers in colleges. However, the available evidence does not seem to suggest that these characteristics are prerequisites for improving achievement. Specifically, there is substantial evidence that:

- Student achievement can be improved by the application of reasonably well-known pedagogic principles in the classroom and workshop (Creemers, 1994).
- Teachers can be supported and developed in the practical application of these principles (Martinez, 1999b).
- Student success depends ultimately on a partnership between student, teacher and college with a range of support staff and managers working closely with teachers (Martinez, 1999a).

Golden rules to improve achievement

The final, and perhaps the most deeply rooted, assumption of all is that there are 10 golden rules to promoting student achievement and that such rules can be applied to any group of students, on any course, in any college. The five 'platinum steps', or the 15 'key priorities', are versions of this assumption.

These are at best half-truths. Some generalisations do emerge from the college experience gathered in this research. The problem is that the means of applying and implementing such generalisations will be highly context specific.

Colleges have developed strategies that differ widely in their priorities, content, scope, levels of resourcing and pedagogic assumptions. Indeed, strategies in different areas of the curriculum can often look quite different within the same college.

This is not to espouse an anti-theoretical stance which privileges empirical and concrete experience above all else, but rather to argue that:

- Raising student achievement involves a number of complex and subtle issues.
- The art of improving achievement requires the ability to apply and adapt general principles in specific contexts.
- Teachers, managers and support staff need to be actively engaged in the process of learning about and reflecting on student learning.

Key points

- Student achievement is a hotly contested and controversial subject that inspires strongly held beliefs and some myths.
- The views that raising achievement is not compatible with widening participation or improving retention are not supported by the evidence.
- Available evidence also contradicts the belief that demographic factors (such as social class) largely determine achievement in colleges.
- Substantial improvements in achievement have been made notwithstanding the different degrees of difficulty associated with different subjects, syllabi or awarding body.
- It is the application of reasonably well-known principles of teaching, curriculum design and management, rather than the charismatic personalities of individual teachers or principals, that have the most effect on achievement.
- There is no universal remedy or hard-and-fast set of rules. The development and implementation of strategies are highly specific to the context of the college, department and often the course itself.

3 Student motivation

There is a general consensus among education researchers concerning the importance of student motivation. Writers distinguish between two types of motivation:

- Extrinsic: associated with factors outside the student such as praise, support, exhortation, encouragement, and rewards from others.
- Intrinsic: where the factors that inspire motivation have been internalised in the form of self-belief, confidence, self-awareness and so on (Crowder and Pupynin, 1993; Kember, 1990).

It is usually accepted that intrinsic motivation is:

- Higher or deeper, or more powerful than extrinsic motivation
- Not innate but can be acquired, developed and also lost or undermined
- Developed by experiencing and reflecting on successful learning (Petty, 1998; Mortimore, 1999; Biggs and Moore, 1993; Fallow and Ahmet, 1999).

All of the strategies developed by colleges pay some attention to student motivation. Several were directed more or less explicitly towards encouraging extrinsic motivation. The majority were directed at developing intrinsic motivation through a variety of means including formative value added, tutoring, teaching and assessment strategies and curriculum design. These approaches are examined in later chapters. Several small-scale and more experimental initiatives are reviewed here. The motivational strategies reviewed include:

- Extrinsic motivation:
  - Prizes and ceremonies
  - Parental involvement
  - Student contracts
  - Discipline procedures.

- Intrinsic motivation:
  - Peer support
  - Empowering career choice
  - Careers guidance
  - Career relevant programmes
  - Self-monitoring of attendance.

Strategies to develop extrinsic motivation

Rewards take a variety of forms: from vouchers, award ceremonies and the inclusion of standard items in references (Hartlepool) to prize-giving ceremonies at Winchester Cathedral (Sparsholt). At Uxbridge, incentives for foundation level GNVQ students include structured residential experiences, regular award ceremonies and the recognition of student abilities through their involvement as guides in college open days and in staff association events. At East Birmingham, the Lord Mayor of Birmingham has presented awards and certificates. Bury College presents certificates for good attendance, which have proved popular, along with vouchers for refectory items – which have proved even more popular!

Such ceremonies are aimed in part at parents. Most colleges have taken steps to develop closer relationships with the parents of younger, full-time students and have enlisted their support in motivating their sons and daughters. Specific examples include:

- Introductory days for parents (Bury)
- Inviting parents to interviews and providing information about college expectations, progression opportunities, student workloads and the current system of qualifications (Oxford, Hartlepool)
- Involving parents in discussions with careers advisors (Oxford)
- Informal early parents evenings to explore qualifications and present parent packs over tea and biscuits (South Nottingham)
- Reporting student progress to parents (Hartlepool, Runshaw, Oxford)
- Inviting parents to tutorials where 'serious concern' action plans are due to be developed and to any disciplinary meetings (Hartlepool)
- Holding induction events for parents in October where they meet personal tutors, discuss how their children have settled into college, put a face to a name and discuss performance, targets and action plans (Runshaw)
- Contacting parents if the first half-termly review suggests that a student may have problems (Winstanley)
- Holding parents' evenings in October of the first year to explain minimum acceptable grades followed by four parents' evenings over the two years of an A-level programme (Winstanley)
- Offering meetings to the parents of all full-time students during the first term (Canterbury)
- Carrying out more active monitoring of attendance and following up non-authorised absence with parents (Regent College, Arnold and Carlton College).

Almost all colleges have developed some type of contracting arrangements by which students agree to the reciprocal rights and obligations between themselves and the college. Such agreements are commonly termed learning agreements. Hartlepool College has created a succinct but very explicit process to address and identify problems of low expectations and poor attendance on the part of some students. The process involves:

- Discussing and agreeing norms for behaviour
- A student requirement to contact the college in the event of absence
- An undertaking by the college to refer to attendance in all college references and testimonials
- Withdrawing records of achievement and the payment of local education authority (LEA) minor awards or access funds in the event of an unacceptably high level of unauthorised absence
- A three-stage disciplinary process that proceeds from verbal to written warning to suspension
- Reciprocal obligations on the part of the college, teachers and tutors.

Other colleges (Bury, Tower Hamlets) have also streamlined and formalised their discipline procedures in parallel with efforts to support and empower students.

Strategies to develop intrinsic motivation

Peer support

It has long been recognised that developing and providing support to your peers can help to develop intrinsic motivation. Universities have shown substantial interest in peer mentoring and tutoring (Dolan and Cantley, 1998), but this topic has received relatively little attention in writing on further education. Notable exceptions to this observation are contained in the work by Petty (1998) and the review of work at Lambeth College in Martinez et al. (1998). The case study from Palmer's College illustrates a peer mentoring approach. Other examples can be found in later chapters on teaching strategies and curriculum design.

Case Study 1. Peer consultancy among A-level students at Palmer's College

Problem

Palmer's College is a sixth form college in Essex. An at risk group of students existed within the college whose characteristics included:

- Low self-esteem
- The absence of any ultimate goal
- Poorly developed learning skills
- Feelings of not being in control, of insecurity and of not being liked
- Preferred learning styles that provided a poor match with teaching strategies.

Applied strategy

Students who were most at risk were nominated by departments to join a peer consultancy programme in the Humanities Faculty. The peer consultancy programme involves:

- Recognition of personal strengths and weaknesses in the preferred learning style
- An analysis by students of the skills/learning styles needed for success in their A-level programme
- An analysis of subject requirements in three main areas: factual (e.g. note-taking, knowledge and concepts, filing), processes (e.g. memorisation, active reading, planning and review, time management) and outcomes (coursework and examinations)
- Self-assessment and the creation of personal targets for each of the three areas
- Peer coaching to achieve the targets
- Substantial initial facilitation by the programme leader which diminishes sharply after 10 weeks.

Outcomes

- Students are gaining an average of two points higher than their ALIS-predicted point score.
- Initial scepticism from some teachers has turned into a general acceptance of the principle.
- The programme has been extended more widely within the Humanities Faculty to include students who are not on the at risk register and is being taken up by other faculties.
- The programme has grown in size from 22 to around 60 students.
- Peer consultancy is now linked to learning style assessment.

It seems rapidly to be becoming the norm to introduce informal group and team-building exercises in colleges, often as part of induction procedures. Examples of similar strategies adopted by colleges include:

- Team-building on an advanced level engineering programme through outward bound activities (Liverpool)
- Inviting students to nominate a representative to attend course team and subject meetings (Tower Hamlets)
- The introduction of early residential experiences (Liverpool, Lowestoft).

Career relevance

Career relevance is another approach used to promote intrinsic motivation. It involves encouraging students to be clearer in their career objectives and to foster a realistic belief in the achievability of those objectives. The work of three colleges demonstrates different ways to implement this approach.

East Birmingham College has opened a Student Success Centre modelled loosely on a similar unit in its partner community college in Chicago. The main purpose of the centre is to raise aspirations and expectations among the college's inner-city student population. The centre includes:

- Positive images: photographs and text describing previously successful students
- A careers guidance library with information about progression opportunities in further and higher education and employment
- IT facilities with access to job search and careers software packages and a cable link to the local careers service
- Local employment vacancies.

The Student Success Centre is staffed by the college and the local careers service and provides four levels of access: seminars targeted at specific groups of students (for example, pre-vocational students, GNVQ foundation students), self-service, a drop-in advice and guidance service and one-to-one interviews.

There are currently plans to develop the centre further through:

- Greater involvement of current students as role models
- Use of the college intranet
- The creation of a bank of workshadowing and volunteering opportunities.

A key focus is to help students to identify and select career objectives and create plans as to how they might be achieved. A complementary approach has been developed at Basford Hall College. This aims to develop a student's ability to engage with this process and is reviewed in the case study opposite.

Case Study 2. Careers education: Blockbusters at Basford Hall College

Problems

- Tensions surrounding recruitment and guidance – students saw interviews as part of a selection process and gave the answers they believed were required rather than engaging in a more open dialogue
- A substantial number of early course withdrawals
- The absence of clear career goals on the part of some students, usually associated with low self-esteem
- Careers education was seen by many teachers and tutors as a 'repair' or 'crisis intervention' service to help put students back on track.

Applied strategy

The solution developed by the college to address these issues is the short career education and guidance programme called Blockbusters. Its main features are:

- Content: team-building, careers education, interview, communications and decision-making skills, developing self-awareness and the job application process.
- Flexibility: the programme can be customised to meet the needs of different curriculum areas; it comprises several mini-modules that can be broken down and delivered separately.
- Accreditation: Blockbusters is accredited through the Open College Network (OCN).
- Collaboration: the programme was developed via a partnership between teachers, guidance and youth workers.
- Interaction: the programme is designed to be negotiated with students and to be delivered in an engaging and participative way.

The programme's objectives are:

- Self-awareness: to help students know about their own strengths and limitations in relation to learning/career opportunities.
- Transition learning: to foster the ability to make appropriate decisions, realise their implications and prepare for the next step.
- Careers information: to know and to be able to assess sources of help, advice and information and to use information appropriately.
- Opportunity awareness: to know what is available in the education, training and employment fields.

Outcomes

- Positive feedback from students
- Increased and more informed use by students of Student Services
- Teachers report improved relationships
- Improved retention on GNVQ foundation courses, from 41% (1997) to 70% (1998)
- Raised student aspirations and increased confidence
- More positive transitions to Level 2 programmes
- Students have a clear focus on goals and career outcomes.

The detailed objectives of the Blockbuster programme are set out in Figure 2.

Figure 2. Blockbuster programme at Basford Hall College

Purpose

To deliver a careers education programme to motivate, focus and retain students of Basford Hall College.

Objectives

By the end of the programme students will:

- Have selected and structured their own programme of learning within defined parameters
- Have an increased awareness of their strengths and weaknesses in relation to their interaction with others
- Be able to describe key influences on their choices, including the effects of:
  o Stereotyping
  o Gender
  o Racism
  o Sexuality
  o Relationships

- Have a positive and realistic sense of self in relation to career choice and lifelong learning
- Be aware of the variety of future lifestyles and roles and have an understanding of the role of planning in enabling them to achieve their preferences
- Have compared their own abilities with those required within the labour market
- Be able to describe the process of making well-informed, realistic decisions, taking account of:
  o Own values and values of significant others
  o Influences
  o Responsibilities
  o Opportunities available

- Have enhanced their communication skills and be able to present themselves in a positive manner via:
  o CVs
  o Letters
  o Interviews

- Be able to evaluate their progress through the programme and provide feedback on this to course leaders, tutors and peers.

The Student Success Centre at East Birmingham College was developed and led by guidance staff; the Blockbusters programme at Basford Hall College was developed through a partnership between teachers, guidance and youth workers. The third example was developed by a teaching team.

At Wirral Metropolitan College, the Leisure and Tourism team has put in place a variety of strategies relating to attendance, assessment redesign and the development of personal tutoring. The team also developed measures to help advanced and intermediate GNVQ students to clarify their career goals and to emphasise the relevance of their programmes to the achievement of such goals. The main elements of this strategy included:

- A Career Focus Week instead of the first-year work placement (Advanced GNVQ)
- A Careers Forum Day to provide a variety of career ideas within Leisure and Tourism, and involving several local employers
- The creation of an individual career action plan for each student.

The Careers Focus Week included two work placement visits, the shadowing and questioning of a range of staff, the completion of a mock job application and interview, video recording of the interview and feedback to students and a follow-up career interview.

The career action plans provide an opportunity to clarify goals and negotiate actions in a focused way. An example of a career action plan is given in Figure 3.

Figure 3. Wirral Metropolitan College: an example of a career action plan for a student on a Leisure and Tourism Advanced GNVQ

Career goal: overseas representative and/or children's courier		
Skills and experience required in addition to main qualification	**Priority**	**Action to be taken**
Ability to speak foreign language	3	Additional unit offered in 2nd Year GNVQ Leisure & Tourism Course
First Aid Certificate	5	Additional unit offered in 2nd Year GNVQ Leisure & Tourism
Experience of dealing with customers and customer complaints	1	Gained through part-time work in the retail sector
Experience of representative work	2	Personal contact with family friend who has a full-time job as resort rep. in a Spanish hotel. The hotel owner has agreed in principle to the student shadowing the rep. for a two-week period, during the second year of GNVQ course. Financial assistance to be negotiated to support some travel and subsistence costs.
Experience of working with children	4	Gain experience working voluntarily at a children's playscheme run at a nearby school during the summer holidays.

Students discuss with their tutor the type of experience and skills they will need to achieve their career goal and which complements their GNVQ. The student negotiates with the tutor how the action plan could be achieved. As the example demonstrates, this might be through part-time or voluntary work; it might be through additional GNVQ units or other courses. The student and tutor agree the level of support that will be provided by the college and draw up what is, in effect, a contract.

Self-monitoring of attendance

Strategies to improve intrinsic motivation are closely allied to formative value added, tutoring, teaching and curriculum strategies. An underlying theme in all these approaches is to support students as they take more responsibility for their own learning.

Strategies to monitor and follow up attendance issues are widespread and have been reviewed elsewhere (Martinez, 1997). Several colleges in this study are using attendance policies to increase intrinsic motivation.

At Bury College, attendance is self-recorded and monitored by other students. Intermediate students on the Leisure and Tourism course at Wirral Metropolitan College record lateness and absence as part of a pilot scheme. At the end of each semester, students calculate the percentage of sessions that they have attended to date and this is verified by their tutor. Average attendance of all but one student rose to 90% on this programme. A similar process is in place at Sutton Coldfield College as part of the college's formative assessment arrangements.

Key points

- Colleges are seeking to increase achievement via strategies that promote extrinsic and intrinsic student motivation.
- Strategies to increase extrinsic motivation include prizes and ceremonies, parental involvement and student learning contracts and (the often associated) disciplinary procedures.
- Efforts by colleges to increase intrinsic motivation are mostly connected to curriculum design, teaching, formative assessment and tutoring.
- Some colleges are experimenting with specific interventions to enhance intrinsic motivation through peer support, to empower students in their career choices and to develop the career relevance of programmes.
- Monitoring and following up attendance often forms part of strategies to increase extrinsic motivation. Some colleges are experimenting with student self-monitoring of attendance.

4 Value added

Value added approaches have attracted a great deal of interest in recent years from different groups of stakeholders and for different reasons:

- Students are mainly interested in formative value added as a means of assessing their own progress.
- Teachers are interested in both formative and summative value added: formative to monitor student progress; summative as a source of evaluative information about the success of their teaching strategies.
- Curriculum managers tend to focus on summative value added as a means of comparing performance between courses and between faculties or departments.
- College strategic managers and inspection and funding authorities are mainly interested in summative value added insofar as it provides a yardstick to measure institutional effectiveness.

In this context, value added is defined as the comparison between input measures of student attainment at the commencement of programmes (such as GCSEs) and output measures of student attainment at the end of such programmes (such as A-levels), while:

- Formative value added means establishing target grades (minimum acceptable grades or target minimum grades) from input measures and reviewing student progress against such targets.
- Summative value added is the comparison of the grades achieved with the predicted grades.

To date, value added methods have worked best in the comparison between A-level outputs and GCSE inputs where around 50% of the A-level grade can be accounted for or attributed to the student's GCSE scores (Fitz-Gibbon, 1997; DfEE, 1995; Barnard and Dixon, 1998). A FEDA project to investigate the relationships between GCSE scores and GNVQ outcomes and those of GNVQ precursors is underway but will not report for several months.

Bearing in mind these limitations, two main approaches to value added can be identified:

- Formative and summative approaches based on reasonably robust statistical data in the A-level curriculum
- Formative value added in vocational qualifications without any significant statistical underpinning.

A-levels

Value added applications in the A-level curriculum are divided into two approaches: ALIS (A-level Information System) and ALPS (A-level Performance System). ALIS, based at the University of Durham, receives data from several hundred colleges and schools and compares A-level grades with average GCSE grades, subject by subject. The advantages of ALIS are that it is based on a large sample, on work that has been taking place over a number of years and it addresses directly the issue of subject difficulty.

ALPS was developed by Greenhead College (and is sometimes known as the Greenhead Model). In contrast to ALIS, it is premised around an analysis of a college's own data to establish a baseline position and then, by a process of incremental improvements, to improve on the baseline position. To derive useable statistics from a much smaller data set, ALPS treats A-levels as being of equal difficulty and usually calculates average GCSE scores more simply than the calculation that underpins ALIS (Conway, 1997).

The advantages of ALPS are that a college remains in control of its own data and there is no subscription fee, as there is with ALIS. A disadvantage is that it deals with fewer variables.

Both ALIS and ALPS have their supporters. What is clear is that:

- Both approaches seem to work
- Both have been key elements in raising A-level achievement in a number of colleges
- The use of value added analysis in A-levels – at least for full-time 16–19-year-old students – is rapidly becoming the norm in colleges and school sixth forms.

For further discussion of value added methods see Conway (1997), Spours (1996) and Spours and Hodgson (1996).

The colleges included in this research have derived a number of learning points about value added, as outlined below.

Student motivation

- The accurate and realistic prediction of A-level grades is a better stimulus to action than encouragement targets.
- As far as students are concerned, the focus is not the comparison between their individual performance and that of the group or class but rather on how far they have travelled and what steps they need to take to arrive at their destination.
- Students generally are interested in predicted grades; students with poor or moderate predicted grades tend to be reassured and stimulated rather than put off or demotivated.
- Targets and progress towards such targets provide the basis for a focused exchange with parents as well as with students.

Teaching and tutoring

- Although value added is premised on data, one of its most important aspects is the relationship between student and personal tutors who know their students, champion their interests and liaise closely with subject tutors.
- Value added methods challenge tutors to become diagnosticians: to determine how students can develop and demonstrate their skills and to identify the specific actions the individual student needs to take.
- Value added helps to identify students at risk of underperforming in a specific subject or across all their subject choices.

Curriculum management

- Value added approaches help to identify where particular strengths or weaknesses occur either in subjects generally or in teaching or curriculum design within a particular subject.
- Value added analyses can inform a review and revision of entry criteria.
- Analysis of value added outcomes by subject and by teacher can increase teachers' understanding, allow them to learn from successful practice and identify and address problems.
- Such analysis provides a practical and pragmatic research focus for colleges.

Implementation

- Students need to retain ownership of their action plans and these need to be revised at least once and more probably twice a term.
- GCSE data from schools is sometimes under-recorded and colleges may need to undertake their own data collection.
- Staff development is important to support the initial implementation of value added and subsequently to ensure that good practice is shared internally and can be identified and brought back from other colleges or training providers.
- Where value added methods have been implemented across the whole of an A-level curriculum, this has required hands-on management that involves celebrating students' success and sometimes challenging existing practices.
- Systems and procedures are required to underpin all of the items listed above.

Summing up his college's experience of formative value added over several years, Principal of Greenhead College, Kevin Conway said:

> *The whole process is very warmly welcomed by students and staff. It has broken down barriers very quickly, and has led to a greater confidence in students to approach staff at any level, if problems arise.*
>
> *It is the realisation of the college's principles that everyone is an exception, and individual and is to be valued. It is the ether that develops the college in an ethos of warmth and support as well as intellectual challenge. (Conway, 1997)*

Vocational qualifications

Until robust relationships can be determined between input measures and outcomes, value added methods in vocational qualifications will not have the same statistical underpinning as in A-levels. Summative value added calculations, in particular, to explore departmental or institutional performance will not be meaningful.

However, formative value added has been championed by the Institute of Education for a number of years (Spours, 1996; Spours and Hodgson, 1996) and several colleges are reporting encouraging results in vocational qualifications.

As might be anticipated, approaches differ widely between institutions in terms of their scope (what is to be measured) and the degree of quantification involved in the measurements.

As part of its Unified Tutorial System (see next chapter), Hartlepool College has introduced an indicative grade for overall progress that is determined by the personal tutor at the conclusion of the termly one-to-one review meeting with students. The grades are:

A. Excellent progress against all targets
B. Generally good progress against all targets
C. Generally satisfactory progress
D. Good progress but with difficulties in some subjects
E. Cause for concern: attendance hindering progress
F. Cause for concern: other factors hindering progress
G. Serious concern: attendance
H. Serious concern: other factors.

Any of the 'concern' grades (E–H) require students to agree a specific action plan with their tutor.

Sutton Coldfield College has developed a more detailed system: STAR (Student Tracking and Achievement Record). This aims to engage students in a review and discussion of their progress, to look at progress from a holistic point of view and to get students to take more responsibility for their learning. Tutors at the college have identified characteristics of successful students. Characteristics of success and failure have been turned into a self-assessment instrument for use by students, which can be adapted for different programmes. The first self-assessment takes place within the first five weeks of the course and then at termly or twice-termly intervals thereafter. Students evaluate their performance against criteria such as attendance, the creation of a time management plan, hours of part-time work per week, hours of independent study per week and so forth. The tutor validates the student's self-assessment, for example by referring to registers, and helps the student to review progress and set targets.

The self-assessment instrument for GNVQ programmes is shown in Figure 4. The comparable instrument for GCSEs is shown in Figure 5.

Figure 4. Successful student profile

Managing your time and making the best use of your learning resources

Date:_____ Student name:_____ Tutor name:_____

	Weekly attendance for all classes	Punctuality for all classes	Work submitted to deadlines	Private study per week	College LRC private study per week	Maths additional support (if applicable)
Achieve	100%	100%		12	6	100%
	95%	95%		10	5	95%
	90%	90%	100%	8	4	90%
Non-achieve			75%	6	3	12
			50%	5	2	18
				4	1	24
				3	0	26

	English-additional support (if applicable)	Part-time employment hours per week	Social life (evenings out) per week	Hours spent in amenity block per day	Effective time management plan in place	
Achieve	100%	3	1	0·5		
	95%	6	2	1		
	90%	9	3	1·25	Yes	
Non-achieve	4	4	1·5			
	5	5	2			
	6	6	3		No	
	7	4	4			

Minimum target: 9 categories of achievement (compulsory)

+ 2 categories of achievement (if applicable)

*On target *Close to target *Off target (*Delete as appropriate)   Student's result: _____categories of achievement

Figure 5. Successful subject profile

Sutton Coldfield College

STUDENT NAME: _____

TUTOR NAME: _____

Date: _____

SUBJECT: _____

(The best ways to reach a PASS standard in each of your subjects)

	Standard of Presentation	Complete set of notes	Homework (Hours per week)	Classroom contributions to discussions	Essay/Average assignment/test grades	Deadlines met for submitting coursework	Talking in class/ Distracting other students	Concentration in class	Predicted grades
ACHIEVE	Excellent	Extra notes	Over 3.0	Always	A/Distinction	100%	Never	Excellent	A/Distinction
	Very Good	Some extra notes	3.0	In most classes	B/Merit	95%	Hardly ever	Very good	B/Merit
	Good	Complete set	2.5	Frequently	C/Pass	90%	Rarely	Good	C/Pass
NON ACHIEVE	Fair	Several pages of notes missing	1.5	Sometimes	D/Referral	Below 85%	Sometimes	Fair	D/Referral
	Poor	Many pages missing	1.0	Rarely	E/Fail	Below 50%	Often	Poor	E/Fail
			None	Never		Coursework	Always		

* On target
* Close to target
* Off target
* Delete as appropriate

APPROVED/NOT APPROVED FOR EXAMINATION ENTRY (Delete as applicable)

Minimum Target: **9 categories of achievement**   Student's Result: _____ **categories of achievement**

Tutor: _____

STAR FORM 3

Two other colleges within the sample have developed value added approaches for vocational qualifications. Runshaw College has introduced target minimum grades for all full-time students across vocational and academic programmes. These are recorded on the student record card and used regularly to review progress. Over a typical two-year programme, targets will be reviewed and updated some nine times and three reports will be generated for parents.

At Barnfield College, value added has been used with some success in vocational programmes both formatively (primarily for students) and summatively (as a means for teaching teams and managers to review performance).

The college first explored the issue in 1995 through an internal research project which examined 26 courses and 650 students. It found that many students had little understanding either of their own progress or of their likely success of achieving a qualification. Take-up of additional support was poor and, as a result, the outcomes of initial testing were poor predictors of student achievement.

After three years of incremental change, targets are now set for all students on full-time vocational courses based on entry qualifications, the need for additional support and ongoing student coursework. Every seven weeks, student progress is monitored and reviewed. Teaching teams are encouraged to review and evaluate their own performance by reference to student outcomes against predictions, and other selected indicators including the numbers of exceptional entry students, the take-up of additional support, retention data and ethnicity.

In common with other formative assessment processes, value added can promote extrinsic and intrinsic motivation, discussed in the previous chapter. As students internalise standards, develop learning skills and become more adept at using value added feedback, initial extrinsic motivation (progress towards a qualification) seems to be increasingly supplemented by intrinsic motivation (habits of success).

Value added, formative assessment and student profiling

This brief exposition raises the question of whether the types of value added approaches adopted in vocational qualifications are a stop-gap substitute for the more statistically based methods developed in A-levels.

It seems more likely that the two should be seen as complementary. The A-level approach is statistically robust and has a reasonably good predictive power but does not on its own shed much light on the process or behaviours that give rise to differing degrees of student progress. The student profiling approach is the opposite: its predictive power may be low, but it can provide a rich picture of student progress. The ideal might be to combine both approaches. The worst-case scenario, to be avoided at all costs, would be a perception of a student's progress on the part of student, tutor or both, which is vague or inaccurate. Figure 6 suggests the relationship between these two approaches.

Figure 6. Value added: relationship between predictive power and qualitative information

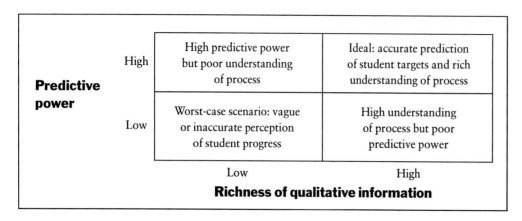

Key points

- Value added approaches are proving popular with students, parents, teachers and curriculum managers.
- The aspects of value added approaches that are particularly effective include setting and reviewing target minimum grades, monitoring and action planning student progress and using the information to inform the management of teaching and the curriculum.
- The use of value added approaches is becoming increasingly widespread in the A-level curriculum and, in some colleges, is associated with substantial improvements in A-level achievement.
- Colleges are making use of both nationally available (ALIS) and home-grown (ALPS) approaches.
- Colleges have experienced difficulties in trying to extend similar methods to vocational qualifications, notably GNVQs.
- Some colleges have pioneered formative value added processes and student profiling.
- Formative value added approaches in relation to vocational qualifications seem to have beneficial effects notwithstanding the absence of a firm statistical underpinning.
- There appears to be some further scope to bring together the statistical value added methods developed primarily in relation to A-levels and the student profiling and formative approaches developed mainly in vocational areas.

5 Tutoring

Evidence shows that effective tutoring plays an important role in improving retention and that the pastoral focus of tutoring is being displaced by an emphasis on monitoring, reviewing and supporting student progress (Martinez, 1997). Tutors have a key role in monitoring and supporting overall student progress, helping students to review and action plan, motivating students and implementing value added approaches. Research has also shown that effective tutoring helps to raise achievement. As a result colleges have developed a number of strategies to improve the effectiveness of tutorials.

In most colleges all full-time and a significant number of part-time students have a personal tutor. Personal tutors work closely with their tutor group on issues related to attendance, motivation, progress and achievement. The main vehicle for tutoring is the one-to-one tutorial which takes place every five or six weeks for some 15–20 minutes to review student progress and action plan. A high degree of participation by students, and their ownership of the process, are key ingredients of effective tutorials.

Many colleges feel the need to develop, resource and support this type of tutoring model. An illustrative case study from Hartlepool College is set out in Case Study 3 overleaf.

Case Study 3. Tutoring at Hartlepool College

Problems

- Low levels of achievement, perpetuating a culture of low achievement at school
- Inconsistent tutorial provision between departments
- Many students and some tutors saw tutorials as being only for students with problems, informal and reactive (offered on a drop-in basis only)
- Tutorials were not cost-effective: they took up 8% of available teaching hours without a commensurate effect on student achievement
- Too much tutorial time was devoted to data and information gathering tasks.

Applied strategies

The main way in which the college addressed the problems was to set up its Unified Tutorial System (UTS). This involved refocusing tutorials around the monitoring, reviewing and action planning of student progress (one hour per student per term) and a tutorial curriculum (one hour per week), based on careers education and a programme of activities to include work experience, residentials, voluntary work, key skills attainment etc.
The main features of the system are:

- A recognition that tutoring requires specialist skills, which will be covered via appraisal, in staff development and at appointment stage
- The establishment of a Senior Tutors Committee, whose terms of reference are:

  To share good practice across departments in order to develop and ensure consistency; to ensure that all policies, including the UTS, are applied consistently across the college; to monitor tutorial provision and report to Senior Management; to advise on staff development requirements

- The redeployment of existing support staff into the new role of 'Departmental Administrators' whose job description is:

  To carry out under the direction of senior tutors all of the administrative tasks that support the tutor's functions: processing examination entries, completing enrolment formalities, chasing up student questionnaires, preparing review packs, processing absences, end-destination data etc.

- A tutor development programme that covers:
  - Interviewing skills
  - Reviewing and action planning
  - Dealing with challenging behaviour
  - The structure of the UTS
  - Careers education
  - The taught tutorial programme
- Student progress reports being held on the college intranet so that they are available to course tutors.

Continued opposite

Continued from page 30

Outcomes

● A substantial improvement in achievement rates:

Figure 7. Achievement rates at Hartlepool College (1995 and 1997)

	1995	1997
GNVQs and precursors	68%	79%
All NVQs	79%	89%
GCE A/AS-level	54%	75%
GCSE	43%	56%
Other	69%	81%

● An 8% increase in attendance rates
● An improvement in retention rates to above average for FE colleges.

Reading College and School of Art and Design addressed a similar set of issues by creating senior tutors responsible both to their head of faculty and to the student services manager. Their main role was to address inconsistencies in tutoring, share good practice, and help tutors in their respective faculties to develop practical strategies to improve retention and achievement. A development programme was introduced for tutors (three days per year) and teaching observation was extended to tutorials.

Great Yarmouth College has made similar efforts to clarify the purposes and expectations of tutors and students and tighten up quality arrangements. The college's ISO 9000 registration now includes tutoring and the litmus test for quality is whether 'the weakest tutor in the college is tutoring effectively'.

Perhaps the most radical approach in terms of structure and systems, out of those reviewed in this study, has been developed at Runshaw College. Full-time students are involved in a 50-minute weekly group tutorial devoted mainly to personal and social education, college information, attendance monitoring and dealing with everyday problems. A second weekly period is devoted to one-to-one tutorials to monitor progress against target minimum grades, and students see their tutors individually every four to six weeks. The college has adopted a 'super tutor' model where tutors may have between 75 and 125 students (organised into three to five tutor groups), but teach correspondingly less. The college has addressed the perennial problems of tutorial focus, standards and quality by creating a structure for tutoring based on a matrix with a strong cross-college element. Schools within faculties are responsible for curriculum delivery, quality and the line management of subject and unit tutors. Three heads of study (for A-levels, advanced vocational qualifications and foundation and intermediate qualifications, respectively) have ultimate responsibility for coordinating quality assurance, personal tutoring and retention, achievement and attendance strategies across the faculty, combining the roles of manager, coordinator and student advocate.

In the examples given above, the emphasis has been on centrally driven tutorial changes, often to address perceived problems of variable practice and tutor uncertainty about the purposes of tutoring. Liverpool Community College found evidence of these problems when it audited its tutoring provision. However, it also found many examples of good practice that had been developed by tutors in different curriculum areas. These included:

- Careful planning and timetabling (Business and Technology Education Council (BTEC) National Diploma in Electronics)
- Accredited tutorial portfolios (Access to Higher Education)
- Basic counselling skills as part of the tutorial curriculum (NVQ Advanced Care)
- Career and time management planning (BTEC Business and Finance)
- Information technology (IT) study skills packages (BTEC National Diploma, Popular Music).

Students were unanimous about the importance of tutorials. Some said that the opportunity to review their individual progress, discuss careers and further education and training opportunities or develop study skills had been an important motivator to remain on their course (Liverpool Community College Courier, 1998).

Key points

- Tutoring is central to most college strategies to raise achievement.
- The largely pastoral focus for tutorials in some colleges is giving way to an emphasis on monitoring, reviewing and supporting overall student progress.
- Key elements in most tutoring systems include one-to-one tutorials, the skills and competencies of effective tutors and supportive administrative and managerial systems.
- Strategies to develop and improve tutoring are often centrally driven and contain a strong student services element.
- One of the main priorities for many colleges has been to improve the quality of tutoring by such means as staff development, role clarification, tutorial observations, improved administrative support and better cross-college coordination.

6 | Teaching and pedagogy

There is a paradox around teaching and pedagogy. On the one hand there is a growing conviction across the FE sector that teaching and pedagogy are particularly important and will be at the heart of efforts to raise achievement. On the other hand, there is little consensus about what will work best and little empirical evidence to support different viewpoints. Teaching approaches based on information and communications technology, key skills, learning styles, active learning, resource based learning, open learning, and so on, all have their different proponents. Yet there is no feeling of certainty about what will work best on a specific course and for a particular group of students.

There is a pressing need to make progress. Put positively, teachers need to be able to access successful practice and feel confident in a developing body of professional knowledge and expertise. Put negatively, the lack of time and resources makes wheel-reinvention an expensive luxury.

In an attempt to derive maximum benefit from the experiences of the colleges in this study, while avoiding the danger of faddism or fashion, this chapter will:

- Summarise empirical research on teaching and pedagogy derived mainly from school effectiveness and school improvement research traditions
- Use case studies to illustrate the diversity of strategies developed in different colleges and curriculum areas
- Discuss the relationship between the findings derived from the schools research and from the case studies.

Teaching and pedagogy have been explored at some length and in some detail in debates around school effectiveness and school improvement (Sammons *et al.*, 1997; Somekh *et al.*, 1999; Brighouse and Woods, 1999; Joyce *et al.*, 1999). This and the following chapter (on curriculum strategy) are based firmly on experiences from case study colleges, from which general inferences are drawn. The case studies have been selected to cover a variety of programmes and students at different levels, in academic and vocational courses and across a range of curriculum areas. Five of the case studies are set out in this chapter and a further five are included in Appendix 3. Case studies that relate specifically to adult, part-time students are included in Chapter 8.

Messages from education research

There is now a substantial body of empirical research on the effectiveness of teaching. This research has largely been conducted in the schools sector. So drawing conclusions for the college sector needs to be done cautiously given that colleges are distinguished from schools by their size, the complexity of their curriculum and the varied and voluntary nature of their student populations.

Four meta-studies are particularly relevant. They are meta-studies in that each is based on a synthesis of some hundreds of research studies, some of which are, in turn, syntheses of smaller scale studies.

The earliest (Wang *et al.*, 1993) anticipated a number of conclusions made independently in *9000 voices* (Martinez and Munday, 1998). The variables that are closest to the student experience of teaching and learning will have the greatest impact on their achievement. The four 'proximal' variables highlighted by Wang and colleagues were:

- Student-teacher interactions
- Classroom management and instruction
- Student cognitive and psychological variables
- Student home environment.

The most extensive and detailed meta-study to date (Creemers, 1994) drew broadly similar conclusions. Insofar as education systems can affect student achievement, classroom level interactions will have the greatest impact. From an exhaustive study of the literature, Creemers identified three main types of variable associated with student achievement: curriculum, grouping and teacher behaviours.

Curriculum variables included the structure of the curriculum and the clarity of its content, the explicitness and ordering of goals, advanced organisers (i.e. making links with what pupils already know and identifying what they will learn next), materials to evaluate student learning, processes and structures for feedback and the availability of corrective instruction.

Grouping variables included the ways that students were grouped in forms or sets or for specific tasks, cooperative learning groups, differentiation, adaptive teaching (that which is adapted to the evolving needs of students) and mastery learning (briefly: clarity in learning objectives, small units of learning, frequent testing, prompt feedback, clear instructions for improvement, and optimising time available to learn).

The most effective teacher behaviours included: classroom management, the regular setting and marking of homework, high expectations of students, clear goal-setting, well-structured lessons, clarity of presentation, questioning of students, immediate exercises for students to apply their learning, evaluation of student progress, feedback, and corrective instruction.

A more recent meta-study (Scheerens and Bosker, 1997) looked more broadly at the literature and research on educational effectiveness. The authors found a broad agreement around some 13 factors that enhanced school effectiveness, 10 of which occurred wholly or mainly at the classroom level:

- High teacher expectations of students and a focus on the mastery of basic subjects
- Quality of the curriculum and, in particular, opportunities to learn and apply learning
- School climate: an orderly atmosphere; clear rewards and sanctions; engagement of pupils in their learning; the quality of relationships between teachers and pupils
- Evaluative potential: monitoring pupil progress and making use of the results of evaluations of student learning
- Classroom climate: relationships in the classroom
- Effective learning time: time at school; time in the classroom; time on task; homework; the monitoring and follow up of absenteeism
- Structured teaching: lesson structure; lesson preparation; direct instruction; regular checking of student progress
- Encouragement of independent learning among students
- Differentiation
- Reinforcement and feedback.

Available quantitative evidence suggests that the factors that have the greatest impact on student achievement are associated with efforts to maximise time on task, structured teaching, differentiation and feedback and reinforcement.

In the most recent meta-study of almost 700 research items, Black and Wiliam (1998) emphasised the particular importance of formative assessment. They found that in some studies, the largest improvements in learning were associated with improved feedback. In this context, feedback and formative assessment are construed broadly to include:

> ... the setting of clear goals, the choice, framing and articulation of appropriate learning tasks, the deployment of these with appropriate pedagogy to evoke feedback [from students] ... and the appropriate interpretation and the use of that feedback to guide the learning trajectory of students. (1998, pp61)

Case studies

The five case studies that follow explore teaching and pedagogy in further education contexts. They provide examples of particular initiatives to give an idea of how some colleges have put these issues into practice and demonstrate the variety and richness of the strategies that are being developed. A further five case studies are included in Appendix 3.

Boundaries between teaching, curriculum design, tutoring, guidance, learning support and such like are rarely clearly defined. The case studies are no exception and as such combine a focus on teaching and pedagogy with references to other types of strategy, showing how teaching and other issues interrelate in specific contexts.

The case studies that present programme or subject specific strategies come first, followed by those developed in a large faculty.

Case Study 4. History department, Solihull Sixth Form College

Problems

- Decline in A-level exam grades (A–E and A–C) from above to below national average between 1991 and 1996
- Achievements in History A-levels below the norm for other subjects in the college
- Average GCSE point scores of history students had remained similar (at around 5·7) over the period.

Applied strategies

- Transfer to modular syllabi which also contained assessed coursework
- Identification of particular learning skills required for success in History A-levels (e.g. essay writing) and creation of pro formas and learning materials to help students develop such skills (examples are given in Appendix 2). Students use the self-assessment pro forma to keep a record of their work, to make their own reflective judgement before receiving feedback and then to make further comment after receiving feedback
- Adoption of a common framework for giving feedback to students: positive initial comments; a maximum of three or four clear instructions for improvement in the next piece of work and a final encouraging comment
- Students given feedback in class and immediately create plans for their next assignment
- Students encouraged to self-assess their work (an example of an assessment sheet is given in Appendix 2·3)
- Differentiation: agreed individual targets and progress reviews supported by ALIS value added predictions for each student; differential tasks at certain stages of the course; challenges for more able students through additional topics; guidance offered to influence student choice of coursework topic; group and project work set as appropriate for the ability groups within a class
- More active teaching strategies: less presentation of information and more pair and groupwork to research and present issues, discussion and preparation of essay plans, and the development of study skills
- A sharply focused revision programme
- More varied pace and tasks in all lessons: tasks included, for example, 'board meetings', balloon debates, role plays, writing articles and editorials, creating diary pages for historical figures, whole class debates, regular short fact tests, mind maps and 'letters to my heir'. Some examples of these are given in Appendix 2.

Outcomes

The outcomes are shown in the data set out in the table below. In summary:

- A–E and A–C pass rates have increased from below to above national average between 1996 and 1998
- The annual intake of students has increased from 139 to 160 (1996–98); average GCSE point scores have stayed the same.

**Figure 8. The average GCSE score for history students at Solihull
Sixth Form College**

Year	Pass rate	National pass rate	Grade A–C	National grades A–C	History students' average GCSE score
1991	87·7	81·1	55·6	49	5·9 (112)
1994	85·6	81·3	54·4	49·4	5·7 (121)
1995	80·6	82·3	45·7	49·6	5·6 (129)
1996	83·6	84·3	46·4	51·1	5·7 (139)
1997	95·5	85·6	72·1	53	5·7 (158)
1998	93·7	86·8	67·3	55·6	5·6 (160)

The Solihull Sixth Form College case study is focused almost exclusively on teaching and learning issues (with some strategies to redesign the A-level History curriculum). Examples of some of the teaching and learning materials are contained in Appendix 2.

The music technology case study from Arnold and Carlton College, which follows, provides a particularly rich illustration of the ways in which teaching strategies can be linked to curriculum strategy; (change of programme offer, timetabling, use of ICT); processess to support achievement (selection and recruitment, initial testing, course transfer, accreditation of prior learning); staff motivation (team development) and resources (accommodation and equipment).

Case Study 5. Music technology programme at Arnold and Carlton College (now part of New College Nottingham)

Problems

- Mismatch between the wants and expectations of some students and the requirements and content of the programme
- Poor retention and achievement (below 50% on some courses)
- Lack of clear progression routes
- Dispersed and poor quality accommodation.

Applied strategies

- Surveyed students who had withdrawn
- Carried out market research to identify progression opportunities and clarify potential markets
- Broadened the range of programmes to include entry and foundation levels
- Improved contacts with industry
- Provided more focused entry criteria; introduced selection into the recruitment process
- Introduced the requirement that tutors make informal contact with students after interview
- Combined workshops, visits, social events and competence tests within the induction process; encouraged students to move between programmes, if appropriate
- Checked after three weeks to ensure that students are on the right course
- Introduced new course content to give students an advantage in the jobs market (e.g. desk-top publishing, 3-D studies, Photoshop)
- Ensured that all students (including part-time) have a weekly personal tutorial
- Consolidated the full-time timetable into two days to facilitate part-time work, and directed private study
- Increased use of ICT: music business and music theory are now taught via computers using the Internet/graphic software/music sequencing software
- Emphasised team-teaching, involving full- and part-time teachers
- Introduced fast-tracking, supported by the accreditation of prior learning
- Improved facilities and equipment, and relocated to a single site
- Involved student representatives in twice-termly team meetings and introduced regular surveys of student opinion
- Developed a culture of reporting absence; at the end of every day follow-up by telephone any non-notified absence with the student (or parents of 16–18-year-olds).

Outcome

Retention and achievement rates have both doubled within a year.

At Barnsley College, strategies developed for GNVQ Art and Design addressed issues relating to teaching and learning (project work, cooperative learning, key skills and action planning). To ensure that these changes were objective, the teaching team also simplified administrative tasks, introduced new or revised processes to support achievement (entry criteria, pre-entry advice and guidance), and condensed the timetable. This strategy is reviewed in the case study below.

Case Study 6. GNVQ Art and Design at Barnsley College

Problems

- Relatively poor retention and achievement rates at intermediate and advanced level
- Poor progression of advanced level students to higher education.

Applied strategies

- Radically restructured GNVQ advanced courses: all mandatory units and part of the optional units were covered in Year 1 and the second year had a focus on special projects with more time devoted to group discussion and criticism, and more time to prepare for progression to higher education or employment
- Clarified entry requirements: four GCSEs at C or above for advanced and between nil and three GCSEs for intermediate entry
- Improved pre-entry guidance to offer greater clarity about course requirements (including, for example, the requirement for maths) and the increased demands of the first year of the advanced programme
- Ensured that key skills specialists support the more realistic integration of key skills
- Condensed the timetable so that both intermediate and advanced GNVQs are run over 3·5 days
- Reviewed action-planning procedures to include student evaluation and grading of own work
- Strengthened internal verification via twice yearly standardisation meetings
- Simplified student paperwork around a single student logbook.

Outcomes

- Retention rates increased from 1995–98 as follows:
  - Advanced Year 1: 61 to 82%
  - Advanced Year 2: 81 to 96%
  - Intermediate: 66 to 86%.

- Achievement rates in 1997/98 were significantly above national average:
  - Intermediate: Barnsley 63%; national 48%
  - Advanced: Barnsley 82%; national 67%.

- 100% of UCAS applications to higher education courses in 1998 were successful.
- The percentage of advanced students progressing to higher education increased from 7% in 1996 to 43% in 1998 and to employment from 17% to 28%, respectively. A corresponding reduction occurred in progression to higher national diplomas (HNDs) and other FE programmes.

One of the most radical set of strategies to improve teaching and curriculum design was developed for Advanced GNVQ in Leisure and Tourism at Lowestoft College. The strategies have been so successful that further changes have been introduced. At the time of writing, the Leisure and Tourism team is planning even more radical changes in order to deliver the whole programme in a single year (but with a substantial increase in teaching time for that year).

The following case study describes the changes that were implemented in the first phase and for the first year of what was still a two-year programme.

Case Study 7. GNVQ Advanced Leisure and Tourism at Lowestoft College

Problem

- Dramatic decline in student outcomes in GNVQ compared with previous BTEC National: from 95% to 54% (retention) and from 95% to 45% (achievement).

Applied strategies

- Changed assessment process to one assignment per unit (in 1994–96 there were 100 pieces of assessed work)
- Provided 'short, fat' mandatory modules, which were delivered and assessed one at a time
- Developed a single scheme of work with clear allocation of responsibilities
- Involved the whole team in the planning and delivery of units
- Introduced a longer induction period (to include team-building)
- Identified at risk students
- Included a practical/study residential (outward bound at Ullswater: 9 GNVQ elements)
- Timetabled in an assessment workshop and attendance over three days per week (12·5 hours per week over 36 weeks)
- All teaching is now carried out by full-time staff
- Made it a requirement that all direct costs are less than 50% FEFC income
- Reduced course hours to 450.

Outcomes

- At June 1999, 100% of the intake (26) was retained; 92% progressed to Year 2 (24).
- All students completed two-thirds of the full award in the first year.
- There were improvements in punctuality and attendance.
- The course team had 2·3 full-time equivalent (FTE) staff, each generating approximately 3500 FEFC units of funding.
- All but one student passed four end-of-unit tests in Year 1.

The four case studies reviewed so far in this chapter analyse strategies which raised achievement (and improved retention) in single programmes or relatively small groups of courses or programmes. In the final case study contained in this chapter, at Oxford College of Further Education, the scope of strategies to improve teaching and learning was larger and included A-level humanities subjects and media studies within a large humanities faculty.

Five further case studies which relate primarily to teaching and pedagogy are included in Appendix 3.

Case Study 8. Department of Languages and Humanities: Oxford College of Further Education

Problems

- Media studies:
  - Poor retention and achievement
  - Insufficient lecturers with direct knowledge and experience of the industry.
- A-levels:
  - Dispersed among four departments
  - Low achievement rates
  - Substantial year-on-year variations in achievement.

Applied strategies

- Media studies:
  - Recruited experienced media practitioners and created fractional posts for people also employed in media-related fields
  - Appointed a curriculum manager with a background in media and the performing arts
  - Introduced two routes: journalism and general/video/film
  - Successfully bid for dedicated facilities and resources
  - Improved the content of assignments, assisted by the external verifier.

- A-levels:
  - Concentrated all full-time humanities A-levels in a home A-level unit within a new faculty structure
  - Adopted mainly modular syllabi
  - Raised entry requirements from four Cs at GCSE to 32 and now 35 points
  - Developed key skills in A-levels with an emphasis on IT as a learning tool
  - Introduced tight interviewing and admissions procedures which determine suitability for A-level study and are continued through August and September
  - Specified certain GCSE grades for particular subjects, e.g. a C in maths to take psychology; a C in English for all subjects
  - Conducted group interviews involving parents and careers advisers followed by individual interviews for different subjects
  - Guided students (and parents) towards BTEC National Diplomas and GNVQs if A-levels were unsuitable
  - Identified at risk students early
  - The first six weeks have an emphasis on identifying learning support needs and checking that students are appropriately placed and are comfortable with their programme
  - Sent twice-yearly reports on student progress to parents
  - Streamlined student tutorial and discipline system.

Outcomes

Figures 9 and 10 show the improvements to achievement and retention by programme type and by subject.

A = achievement and refers to the percentage of students still enrolled and in attendance after 15 May in the year in which the programme ends, who achieved the qualification.

R = retention and refers to the percentage of students enrolled to a programme on 1 November in the academic year in which the programme or the final year of the programme begins, and who were still enrolled and attending on 15 May in the year in which the programme, or the final year of the programme ended.

Figure 9. Humanities A-levels

Two-year programmes	1995/96		1996/97		1997/98	
	A	R	A	R	A	R
Geography	56	90	82	100	100	100
Psychology	71	59	93	83	87	83
English literature	88	97	83	100	96	92
Communications	72	100	100	94	82	100
Sociology	55	92	100	100	93	100
English language and literature	50	100	100	100	81	96

One-year programmes	1995/96		1996/97		1997/98	
	A	R	A	R	A	R
Psychology	65	81	77	87	83	67
English literature	73	76	100	93	100	94

Figure 10. Media programmes

	1995/96		1996/97		1997/98	
	A	R	A	R	A	R
Media A-level 1 year (evenings)	42	86	67	30	83	86
Media GNVQ Intermediate	N/A	N/A	65	77	88	80
Media BTEC HND	86	91	92	100	97	86
Media A-level 1 year (part-time day)	67	90	100	68	84	86

Discussion

Comparing the strategies contained in these case studies with the findings from the largely school-based research reveals a number of interesting points of similarity and difference.

Strategies developed by colleges that are closely related to those identified in schools include:

- Structured teaching involving clear learning objectives for the programme as a whole and for each individual session, a clear and logical sequence of learning activities and assignments, the redesign of assignments to clarify their purpose and align these with learning objectives
- Student-centred formative assessment which includes structured feedback, instruction for improvement, a focus on the individual learner, self- and peer-assessment and value added methods
- Shared student-staff ownership of learning including adaptive teaching, interim evaluations of teaching and student representation at teaching team meetings
- Differentiation through individual learning programmes, periodic individual review and action planning, differentiation by task or assignment, choice of modules (leading to different vocational outcomes), all of which are supported by initial tests, remedial instruction, and resource-based learning.

There are certain strategies that feature prominently in the case studies but not in the school-based research. These are broadly threshold, tutoring and curriculum strategies.

The different emphasis in colleges on threshold strategies is easily explained by the differences between schools and colleges. For most school teachers, recruitment, course placement, induction, and starting pupils off on a programme of learning are seen as relatively unproblematic. Colleges, by contrast, have needed to pay substantial attention to what in Creemers' terminology (1994) would be defined as 'grouping procedures', including:

- Entry criteria
- Initial information and guidance
- Interviewing and selection
- Induction
- Initial assessment.

The relative sophistication of threshold processes developed by colleges may well have some application in schools and, for that matter, higher education.

The role of the personal tutor has no real equivalent in schools. It involves an oversight of the whole of the student's progress, close liaison with subject tutors and teachers, and both pastoral and academic responsibilities. Again, this can be attributed to the need in colleges to develop a close personal and academic relationship between tutor and student in a large institution where the content of student programmes may be extremely diverse.

In terms of curriculum strategies, the case studies have tended to emphasise the degree of discretion and responsibility exercised by teachers in colleges. The scope of college curriculum strategies extends far beyond the choice of learning materials or the sequencing of content or the use of advance organisers, noted by Creemers. Curriculum strategy in colleges involves choices about: alternative syllabi, modularisation, redesign of the curriculum offer, design and implementation of learning support, and the length and shape of the timetable.

As with threshold strategies, the relative sophistication of the role of the personal tutor and curriculum strategies, as revealed by the case studies, may prove to be useful in other education sectors.

There are some strategies that have proved successful in schools but which do not feature greatly in the case studies. These include the use of mastery and cooperative learning strategies and advance organisers. Since these techniques are well documented, tried and tested and, above all, have been found to be particularly successful with lower attaining school students, there is a strong case for some action research to test their use in further education.

The other main difference between the school and college experience relates to the issue of effective learning time. There is a tension in the college case studies. Strategies are in place to make the best use of time available; but the time available has been contracted sometimes to 2 or 2·5 days per week for a full-time student. This is a matter of concern for both colleges and funding authorities and may need to be addressed via policy decisions in relation to the curriculum, student support and funding for full-time programmes.

There are also some teaching and pedagogic issues that are often considered to be important but which are not reflected in school- or college-based research. These would include:

- Teacher enthusiasm
- Varied teaching strategies
- Frequent checks on student learning
- Good subject knowledge
- Teaching materials produced to a high standard.

The fact that these issues are not reflected in the research may suggest that they should be considered as 'hygiene' rather than 'motivational' factors. All teaching should embody these type of practices, but on their own they will not be sufficient to characterise effective teaching, still less lead to improvements in student achievement.

Key points

- Research on school effectiveness suggests that factors within education systems that impact most strongly on achievement are those that are closest to teaching and learning.

- There is a growing body of evidence derived principally from the school sector on the effectiveness of specific approaches to teaching and learning.

- For several years, colleges have been developing their teaching and learning strategies to improve achievement and retention, and a number of case studies are reported in this and other chapters of this guide.

- Teaching does not take place in isolation. The case studies suggest strong links between the review and development of teaching strategies, curriculum design and processes to inform, advise, guide and support students.

- There are a number of similarities between successful teaching strategies in colleges and those reported in the literature on schools; these include structured teaching, student-centred formative assessment, shared student-teacher ownership of learning, and differentiation.

- Colleges are at the leading edge of development in some aspects of pedagogy, notably: threshold and grouping procedures, tutoring and the devolution of curriculum strategy and design to teachers and teaching teams.

- Some successful strategies reported in schools could usefully be explored in colleges, particularly mastery learning, cooperative learning and the use of advance organisers.

- There are some characteristics that are often associated with effective college teaching but are not identified in the case studies and find little echo in the schools research. These include: teacher enthusiasm, varied teaching strategies, good subject knowledge, high quality teaching materials, and frequent checks on student learning. This is not to say that these aspects of teaching or pedagogy are unimportant but it may well suggest that they are necessary but not sufficient.

- Action research conducted along the lines suggested in this and later chapters will go some way to addressing the lack of empirical work to date on effective teaching in tertiary education generally, and in colleges in particular.

7 Curriculum strategy

Curriculum strategy includes key decisions concerning the content, outcomes, processes and structures of the curriculum. Curriculum strategies to improve retention were reviewed in *Improving student retention* (Martinez, 1997) and four main approaches were identified:

- The development of new courses and programmes (following on from a curriculum audit)
- Changes to curriculum structure and timetabling
- Strategies based on the development of learning to learn skills
- Learning support strategies.

Evaluation of many of these strategies indicated that they were helping to raise achievement as well as improve retention. It is not surprising that colleges in this study have developed similar strategies to address issues of achievement.

Development of new courses and programmes

The process of curriculum renewal through the development of new courses and programmes, the repositioning and redesign of existing programmes and the abandonment of others is too well known to require detailed discussion here. (Staff College/FEU, 1994).

Colleges included in this study introduced a variety of new or revised programmes in order to raise achievement. Specifically, a number of them introduced new and often unitised programmes at entry and foundation level, usually accredited through OCNs. Other FEDA research shows that this strategy is common in English FE colleges and represents the main way in which the curriculum has been unitised at present – at least in England (Pierce, 1998). New or revised programmes reported by colleges in the current research included:

- The introduction of OCN accreditation for modern languages (Oxford)
- A pre-foundation programme (Dewsbury)
- OCN-accredited modules for maths and subsequently for a variety of courses at entry level (Dewsbury)
- The repositioning of the music technology programme (Arnold and Carlton, see case study on pp38)
- The development of programmes at four levels for adults returning to learn (Dewsbury)
- A substantial increase in OCN-accredited modules at entry and foundation level (East Birmingham, Basford Hall)
- Customised or specialised programmes to make accredited learning available to non-traditional students (East Birmingham)

- Separate accreditation of key skills achieved through vocationally designed assignments and delivered via ICT (East Birmingham)
- Additional OCN-accredited units to make a teacher training curriculum more flexible (Solihull).

Just as colleges are adding to, revising and developing new courses to raise achievement, they are also withdrawing from some types of provision for the same reason, with GCSEs being one example. The problems of GCSE retake programmes are well known. Students usually retake them to gain the critical number of five A–C passes to gain access to higher education or other career opportunities. In the early 1990s, less than 50% of students who gained between three and five A–C grades in Year 11 were adding any additional A–C grades in subsequent years. In the case of students with only one A–C pass at Year 11, the percentage adding one or more A–Cs after Year 11 was only 10% (Payne, 1995). Attendance and retention are poor for GCSE retake programmes and colleges have been discouraged from offering them on a full-time basis (FEFC, 1997). Colleges included in the present research:

- Abandoned full-time GCSE retake programmes in favour of intermediate GNVQ (Luton)
- Withdrew from a full-time GCSE resit programme (Greenhead)
- Discouraged students from taking full-time resit programmes (West Kent).

Curriculum structure and timetabling

Improving student retention (Martinez, 1997) reported a number of innovations in curriculum structure and timetabling to improve retention. These included:

- Unitisation and modularisation
- The division of the term into blocks for learning and catch-up weeks
- Greater flexibility through open or resource-based learning
- Adjustments to timetabling.

These types of innovations were often associated with improvements in achievement rates as well as in retention. The experience of colleges included in this study tends to reinforce such associations.

At entry and foundation level, a new and unitised curriculum has been developed to cater for the needs of new, returning and largely non-traditional learners. At advanced level many of the colleges adopted modular A-levels to:

- Improve learning and increase achievement
- Enable students to make measurable progress more quickly
- Provide more equitable and more accurate assessments of ability
- Provide greater opportunities for formative assessment
- Lessen the stress on students (even on those who need to resit modules)
- Make revision more manageable.

This move towards modular A-levels is hardly surprising. It accords with the weight of evidence presented to Sir Ron Dearing (DfEE, 1996) and with substantial anecdotal evidence from the FE sector that modular A-levels improve performance among middle- and lower-ability candidates (without prejudicing the performance of the most able).

However, modularisation and unitisation are still quite rare in England (as opposed to Wales and Scotland) across the whole of a college or the whole of a curriculum area. Improvements in retention and achievement following the implementation of a strategy based on unitisation and resource-based learning in the Engineering Department at Solihull College are described in *Improving student retention* (Martinez, 1997). A similar strategy developed in the same college in the teacher education area has also been successful.

Solihull College offers a large number of teacher and training awards extending from Level 1 to postgraduate certificates and NVQ Level 5. A modular three-phase programme has been developed which starts with 'classroom survival' and extends through an information and guidance workshop to a choice between an NVQ and a non-NVQ route, each with prescribed core modules. This is then followed by a flexible third phase which supports both NVQ and academic assessment and accreditation. A diagram representing the three phases is set out in Figure 11.

Figure 11. Teacher trainer accreditation programme

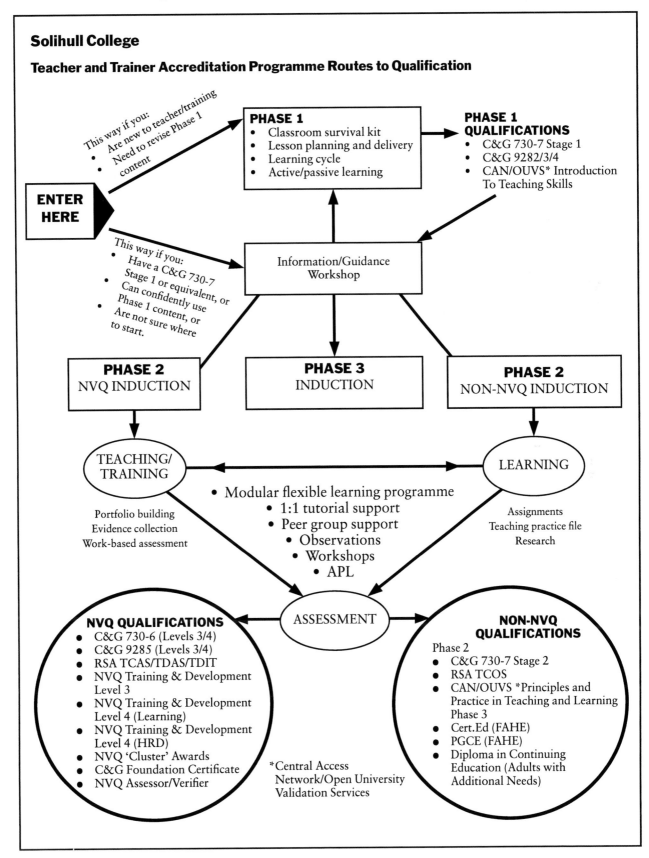

Some students were concerned about the perceived fragmentation of their course. To address this the college adopted a common framework of five-week modules each followed by a week of base-group activity, supported by tutoring. The base groups allowed students to integrate their learning and make sense of practice and theory.

Group teaching has been reduced in favour of a greater emphasis on initial assessment, advice and guidance and the process of planning a programme for each student, workshops, one-to-one tutoring and more varied assessments. Resources derived from savings in classroom teaching time are used to support team and curriculum development. Average retention rates across the teacher development programme are 88% and average pass rates are 90%.

The teacher training department enrols 370 students each year. Around 60% of these students put together a series of modules which very much resemble a conventional course. The other 40% treat the programme flexibly and interrupt and recommence their learning to suit their needs. The flexibility of the programme means that the college can reach out to a greater number of students.

Learning blocks and catch-up weeks

Increasingly, academic terms are being punctuated by periods where the timetable and normal teaching is suspended. In a number of sixth form colleges and in A-level curricula generally, colleges are doing this for a few days per term to allow one-to-one tutoring. Examples of this have already been discussed in Chapter 5. In a number of mainly FE colleges, teaching in specific vocational areas or sometimes across the whole curriculum is suspended every sixth or seventh week. These week-long learning blocks are used for a variety of purposes including:

- One-to-one tutoring
- Residentials/out of college visits/team-building
- Coursework (including opportunities for some students to catch up with coursework and differentiated tasks)
- Individual target-setting
- Collaborative reflection and planning of future tasks
- Identification of at risk students.

The effectiveness of using the time for one-to-one tutoring is relatively easy to demonstrate. It is more difficult to evaluate the impact of the week long learning blocks. One college that is in a position to do so is Telford College of Arts and Technology.

In 1998, the college introduced a model of five-week delivery followed by a sixth learner management week (LMW). This was introduced across all full-time programmes. The aims of the learner management week are to:

- Recognise achievement for progression
- Enhance and pace student experience
- Improve retention
- Ease assessment pressures on students.

The week includes a one-to-one tutorial focused on student progress, aspirations and target-setting. Students use a 'contract planner' to record their plan for the week. Every student has a baseroom, staffed throughout the week. The learner management weeks are staggered across the college.

Learner management weeks also comprise a key element in a programme of change which has included:

- An extensive ILT staff development programme supported by six information and learning technology (ILT) champions and a departmental ILT mentor project
- Sharing good practice through staff bulletins, the college intranet and staff development events

- Significant investment in ILT
- Introducing students to the use of the college intranet as part of their induction to college and creating student e-mail addresses from the second day of their programme
- Witness sessions (to obtain student feedback) convened throughout the year and chaired by the principal and director of curriculum
- Redesigning curriculum delivery models into five or six week blocks
- New schemes of work
- Rescheduling assignment and assessment targets
- Enhancing skills for guidance and counselling to assist at risk students
- Searching for new ways to integrate value added, enrichment, induction activities, learning support and so on.

Outcomes of learning management weeks

- Retention and achievement have improved.
- Staff perceive that the quality of student work is higher.
- Student focus groups have commented favourably on the emphasis on learning and on the contrast with school where 'you are taught all the time'; students value having time to catch up.
- So long as teachers are skilled and committed, the approach works equally well for foundation/intermediate and advanced level courses.

Timetabling

If there is a rough and ready consensus about the use of learning blocks created by suspending the timetable, there is much less agreement about basic issues of timetabling. At one extreme, colleges are running full-time timetables over five days with hours of attendance very similar to those of school. At the other, programmes are being run over two or 2·5 days. *Improving student retention* (Martinez, 1997) suggested that the way in which directed time was structured and the degree of development of students' ability to learn independently were the key issues rather than the pattern and volume of timetabled hours. This now seems too simplistic, since it pays little attention to student needs and characteristics and reduces issues of curriculum and teaching to narrow considerations of the organisation of directed time.

Instead, it seems that successful practice is characterised by timetabling that is determined by the interplay between:

- The needs of students (including needs to earn money or care for others)
- Student learning skills (including time management, cognitive and metacognitive skills)
- Curriculum design
- Teaching strategies
- The nature and level the of learning programme.

This model seems adequate to represent the (largely implicit) decision-making processes that lead to the variety of timetabling outcomes for different courses and different students.

Thus, mature students on an Access course at Amersham and Wycombe are employed, have substantial work-based learning opportunities, have limited time because of work and family commitments but, once their initial anxieties are overcome, have relatively well-developed study skills. A curriculum design modelled on Open University practices and a one evening per week timetable was sufficient to ensure that more than 80% of student starters achieved their qualification aims (Martinez, 1997).

A very different group of foundation level students at Uxbridge College, with poorly developed habits of learning, histories of poor attainment, truanting, illness and behavioural problems required a very different curriculum design and different teaching strategies. These were associated with a full timetable spread over five days and without any substantial gaps in timetable activity (for further details see Case Study 10).

Experiences at Bury and Sutton Coldfield colleges seem to suggest that full-time students on lower level courses will often require a timetable over four or even five days per week; students on higher level courses with more developed learning skills may need less formal teaching.

However, the issue still requires attention and careful negotiation with students to maximise their learning time. Greenhead College has introduced the following procedure to support underperforming students:

> *Provision is made after normal college hours to help students with poor motivation, organisation and study habits. Students under performing contract with their personal tutors to undertake one, two or three evenings per week of study between 3.00pm and 5.30pm in the college library. Contracts are usually made to cover a half-term, but regularly it is the case that students continue to use the system. This is a process of genuine persuasion rather than dictation in the majority of cases. It was begun in 1993 and has had beneficial effects. The added value analysis has allowed us to identify the problem.* (Conway, 1997)

Learning skills and learning support

In many ways, strategies to develop learning skills and embed and extend learning support have anticipated the current drive towards inclusive learning. It is perhaps more helpful and more accurate to see 'learning to learn' and 'learning support' as part of a range of curriculum strategies that reflect an underlying continuum which extends from basic to key skills (FEDA, 1999a). The advantages of this type of perspective are that it is premised on the development of cognitive and metacognitive skills for all students, including students at a variety of levels from entry level to postgraduate.

One of the paradoxes of further education is that the implementation of key and basic skills remains problematic. This is in spite of substantial investments in curriculum and staff development, an impressive degree of professional agreement as to the importance of these issues, and substantial empirical evidence that failure to address basic and key skill needs will lead to drop-out and student failure.

The report on basic education by the FEFC (1998) and the Moser Report (DfEE, 1999) both point to continuing problems of design, implementation and performance. Anecdotes abound concerning students who do not or will not pay sufficient attention to key or basic skills because of lack of motivation, understanding, energy, time, confidence or because of stigma.

For all these reasons, it is worth looking at case study colleges that have raised achievement through learning skills and learning support strategies.

Providing opportunities to develop key skills

In Dewsbury College, screening work done in 1997 and 1998 illustrates a central aspect of this issue: the relatively high proportion of students at all levels with numeracy and literacy skills which are substantially below the level of their programme of study. In 1997/98, of 390 advanced level students who were screened, 6% had reading levels at or below Level 1. An equivalent figure for numeracy was just under 17%.

The college concluded that it needed to provide key skills development opportunities for all students, including those on Level 3 and HND programmes. The main elements of the strategy were to:

- Provide cross-curriculum policies for maths and English
- Introduce a comprehensive programme of targeted additional support in literacy and numeracy

- Develop maths, English and IT study centres
- Introduce accredited programmes of study at all levels
- Develop a number of short modules, for maths in the first instance and accredited by the National Open College Network (NOCN), from Entry Level to Level 2 (see Figure 12).
- Incorporate cross-college timetable slots to ensure that students on all courses have time dedicated to maths, English and IT
- Develop a new programme based around key skills, vocational modules and tutorial/study skills for adult returners at four levels from Entry to Level 3 (Access)
- Create banks of learning materials and assignments
- Review progress formally each term for each key skill.

Figure 12. Dewsbury College: maths provision

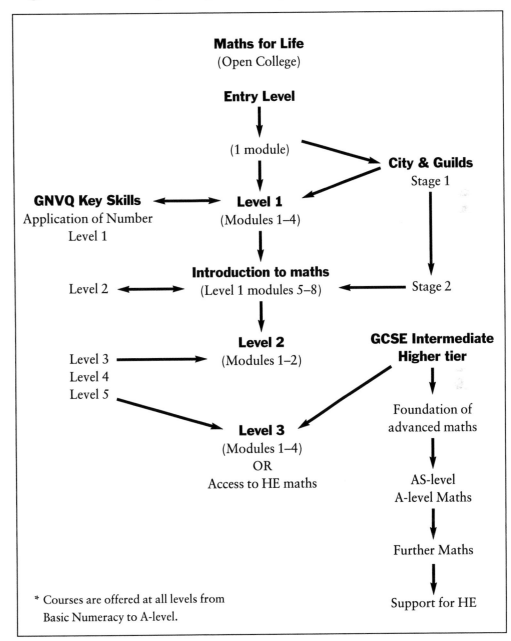

* Courses are offered at all levels from Basic Numeracy to A-level.

Outcomes of strategy

- Around two-thirds of students use the maths study centre beyond their timetabled attendance.
- The college achieved a Beacon Award for maths in 1996 and an inspection Grade 1 for maths in 1994.
- Around 1000 students attend the English and maths centres each week and around 1500 students attend the IT centre.
- A–C pass rates are 55% for GCSE Maths and 67% for GCSE English.
- Pass rates for maths NOCN units are around 95%.

Linking students to learning support

Two years ago, the Basic Skills Agency drew attention to the relatively high rates of drop-out and course failure among students who had basic skills needs but who did not access additional or basic skills support (BSA, 1997). More recently Barking College has found that students who do not get the support they require are 2·5 times more likely to drop out or complete unsuccessfully than students who have the same levels of need but who access learning support. The Barking study also suggests that among students with basic skills needs, accreditation and retention increase with the increasing volume of time spent in the college's key skills centre (Stent, 1998).

This is a widely reported problem and Bridgwater College has designed a number of strategies to address it. These are reviewed in the following case study.

Case Study 9. Learning support at Bridgwater College

Problems

- Lengthy delays associated with centralised administration of initial tests
- The creation of additional support learning programmes were delayed until November or later
- Learning support needs were not being identified outside of Level 1 and 2 programmes
- Poor take-up of learning support by students with identified needs and neglect of learning support issues by some tutors.

Applied strategies

Threshold

- Decentralised initial testing: all curriculum areas must conduct initial assessment of students but how and when is determined by teachers
- Provided a variety of tests including those developed by Construction Industry Training Board (CITB), REMIT, Cambridge Regional College, BSA, Farnborough Technical College and self-devised tests; all tests must be agreed with the college key skills coordinator
- Tightened up exceptional entry rules: all decisions on exceptional entry are made by the head of learner services and teachers have to prepare a case to support any exceptional entrant and indicate how such students will be supported (an example of the college paperwork is given in Appendix 4·5)
- Ensured that all full-time and substantial part-time students (six hours per week or more) are initially assessed
- Identified and monitored the most at-risk (amber alert students) – see pro forma given in Appendix 4·4)
- Included a school report (which identified additional needs) as a routine element of the application process (application form is given in Appendix 4·3).

Delivery models

Three main types of learning support delivery have been developed as follows:

- Integrated: learning support is completely integrated into programmes and ceases to be identified as 'additional' – this applies to all discrete programmes for students with learning difficulties and disabilities, GNVQ and NVQ programmes at Levels 1 and 2, all other courses where common needs are identified for the whole group (e.g. numeracy for performing arts courses) and return-to-learn programmes for adults.
- One-to-one: this support is usually short-term and intensive. It is delivered by additional support staff and reviewed termly; the outcomes of the termly reviews are shared with personal and subject tutors (an example of the documentation is given in Appendix 4).
- Drop-in: drop-in English and maths workshops are used mainly by A-level, higher education and Access to HE students.

At least one teacher in each curriculum team is encouraged to achieve Key Skills Qualifications at Level 4 or 5.

Management

- The head of learner services has been given line management of the learning resource centre, discrete provision and support for students with learning difficulties and/or disabilities (SLDD), senior tutors (who in turn lead all personal tutors), information and guidance and student liaison.
- Staff development and administrative systems have been introduced to identify all learning support costs (a copy of the documentation is given in Appendix 4).

Outcomes

A total of 83% of 101 'amber alert' students on Level 2 programmes completed their programmes (compared to 69% of non-amber alert students). See Figure 13.

Figure 13. Retention and achievement rates at Bridgwater College

	Retention		
	1995–96	1996–97	1997–98
Overall college retention for full-time full-year students	78%	83%	86%
Retention rates for full-time full-year students receiving additional support	82%	83%	91%
	Achievement		
Overall achievement rates for full-time full-year students	80%	81%	82·4%
Achievement rates for full-time full-year students receiving additional support	82%	93%	93·5%

The continuum between strategies to improve basic and key skills can be further illustrated by the Italics Project at East Birmingham College. The college recruits from some of the most disadvantaged areas of inner-city Birmingham and wanted a strategy that would:

● Address the key skills needs of its students
● Integrate key skills with vocational courses
● Attract and motivate students
● Accredit their learning
● Cater for students with key skills needs at Level 1
● Increase achievement.

The solution was the Italics Project which is taught by a key skills specialist heavily supported by ICT and is assessed using vocationally specific assignments. It was piloted in selected vocational areas (hairdressing, business administration and electronic installation). The ICT dimension of the project has proved particularly attractive to students and the project now includes other vocational areas (and has been shared with other colleges in the Heart of England Partnership).

Some learning skills and learning support strategies have been developed specifically for certain groups of students. The Palmer's College peer tutoring and learning to learn approach with A-level students has been discussed above (pp15). Uxbridge College, by contrast, has introduced a radical redesign of its curriculum for Foundation Level. The Uxbridge case study brings together a number of the elements of teaching and curriculum strategies discussed so far to meet the needs of a group of students who often have high drop-out and failure rates.

Case Study 10. Foundation Level at Uxbridge College

Problems

- Three-quarters of all Foundation Level GNVQ students were failing to achieve their qualification aim.
- Foundation level students had very different learning needs and came from a wide variety of home backgrounds including refugees, students with learning difficulties, and students who had missed school because of behavioural and health reasons.
- There were problems developing and coordinating a foundation programme which was located in five different college departments.

Applied strategies

- Introduced initial assessment including formal and informal interviews, BSA tests and more detailed assessments, and personal action planning
- Set up one big programme (about 90 students), located at a single site
- Redesigned the curriculum around key skills (EdExcel Key Skills Award)
- Used other qualifications e.g. RSA achievement tests as stepping stones
- Sequenced achievements after each six or seven week block or set of modules
- Provided a full timetable with no gaps
- Appointed learning coordinators to:
  - Monitor and chase attendance
  - Provide additional tutorial support
  - Help with assignments
  - Monitor work deadlines
  - Support self-study
  - Find work placements

- Provided specialist learning support for individuals and small groups
- Offered structured residential experiences and regular award ceremonies
- Encouraged students to participate in a range of college events e.g. act as guides on open days.

Outcomes

Figure 14. Retention and achievement rates for the Foundation Level GNVQ programme at Uxbridge College

	1995–96	1996–97	1997–98
Retention (%)	50	85	87
Achievement (%)	47	84	100

- Praise from External Verifier
- Foundation programme short-listed for Beacon Award
- Expansion of Foundation Programme
- Increase in the number of learning coordinators

Other strategies to develop and support basic and key skills include:

- Introducing early assignments for diagnostic purposes (Great Yarmouth)
- Training all teachers involved in foundation level programmes in basic skills (Sutton Coldfield)

- Screening all full-time students including advanced level students; this helped to identify a need for maths support for psychology and sociology A-level students (Great Yarmouth)
- Integrating additional support into foundation level programmes (Sutton Coldfield)
- Tightening up all procedures related to the diagnosis of the need for delivery and evaluation of learning support (Barnfield and West Kent Colleges)
- Analysing students' preferred learning style as part of initial assessment using commercially available software (West Kent College)
- Developing a study centre with a similar function to those at Dewsbury (Huddersfield New College)
- Introducing a single study centre catering for the whole spectrum of student learning needs (West Kent College).

Key points

- Curriculum strategies to raise achievement are similar to those developed to improve retention. Specifically, colleges are continuing to review their curriculum offer to introduce new courses and new types of course and to withdraw from inappropriate or ineffective types of provision (even in the face of continuing market demand).
- Other common strategies include: unitisation and modularisation, the division of terms into blocks for learning and catch-up weeks, greater flexibility through open and resource-based learning and adjustments to timetabling.
- Timetabling issues remain controversial, with full-time programmes being arranged over five, four, three and even two days per week.
- A tentative inference is that the management of the teaching week needs to consider five main issues: the needs of students; student learning skills; curriculum design; teaching strategies; the nature and level of the programme.
- Increasingly, colleges are addressing basic and key skills needs as part of a continuum of study skills development rather than as discrete issues. Within such a continuum, substantial effort is being put into diagnosing needs early on, expanding provision to meet identified needs and ensuring that students make optimal use of available support.
- A range of techniques is being used to make basic and key skills support more effective, including integration, contextualisation, additional staffing, enhanced tutoring, monitoring and target-setting, and the training of teachers.

8 | Adult achievement

Issues relating to achievement by adult students are particularly contentious and require some prior discussion before looking at approaches that have proved successful in practice.

Discussions in further, adult and continuing education concerning assessment, accreditation and achievement issues as they relate to part-time adult students are at best ambivalent and at worse contradictory. They almost invariably revolve around the observation that many adult students may not be interested in accreditation or may have had such unhappy experiences of (usually school-based) exams and tests that they are unwilling to submit themselves to any sort of formal assessment. In the words of one recent study:

> *Adult learners do not always, or even mostly, want or need qualifications or formal assessments to achieve their goals or to give value to their achievements.* (Foster *et al.*, 1997)

Similar arguments have been expressed by the Association of Colleges (House of Commons, 1999), the FEFC (1999a, para 25) and Hayes (1999).

This issue goes to the heart of discussions about lifelong learning. It creates a series of potential dichotomies which may be represented as:

- Learning versus assessment
- Informal (and non-accredited) learning versus formal (and accredited) learning
- Learning of interest to students versus accredited (and hence officially sanctioned) learning
- Process (learning) versus outcomes (qualifications).

This is not an idle or abstract philosophical discussion. Unless this issue can be resolved, it promises to undermine any policy to extend, develop and improve lifelong learning since this will inevitably remain divided between largely informal and non-accredited learning ('real' learning so to speak) and the sort of formal and assessed learning which has, so far, been demonstrably unsuccessful in attracting the majority of adults (Kennedy, 1997).

To explore this issue it is first necessary to think more closely about the inspirations, motivations and goals of adult students and to revisit some issues around assessment and accreditation.

Adult student motivation

Some extremely elegant and powerful ways have been found to consider the diversity of part-time adult students. These usually boil down to one of two approaches: the tried and tested socio-demographic models which are premised on age, gender, social class, ethnicity, prior educational experience and attainment (for example, Beinart and Smith, 1998) or psychographic and motivational models based on a mixture of lifestyle, motivational and career-stage or life-stage groupings. To give an example of a psychographic model, Walsall College of Arts and Technology identified four main categories of adult part-time students:

- Early returners
- Late returners
- Improvers
- Enhancers (Martinez, 1996).

Figure 15 shows a highly simplified psychographic model which addresses the alleged dichotomy between learning and qualifications.

Figure 15. Adult part-time students' motivation

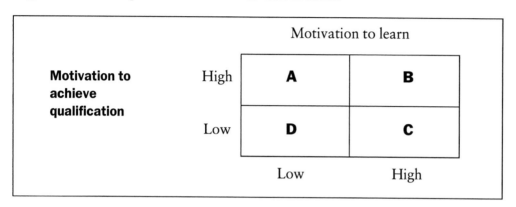

This is a very schematic model which considerably oversimplifies a complex set of issues. Many, if not most, adult education classes may well contain a mixture of students from all four quadrants. It does, however, seem possible to make some cautious generalisations which might help to distinguish student motivations in, for example, a pottery class from those in a class for accountancy technicians.

The students in quadrant A, with a high motivation to achieve and low motivation to learn, might include those who need professional qualifications for career advancement purposes and who have already acquired all the learning they need or who have a largely instrumental approach to the learning required.

Students in quadrant B, with a high motivation to learn and achieve, could include those on return to learn and access courses (to both further and higher education).

Students in quadrant C, with a high motivation to learn but a low motivation to achieve a qualification could include, for example, students on some craft, personal development or foreign language courses.

Students with a low motivation towards learning and qualifications (in quadrant D) might fall into three main groups:

- 'Amenity users' – those who enrol primarily to access facilities or equipment; this group would seem to fall outside the terms of the present discussion since providing a service for people who wish primarily to access facilities could be done in other ways than the provision of a course or programme of study
- Students acting under some form of constraint, such as unwilling students dispatched to courses by their employers; Job Centres or DSS Offices
- Students with very low levels of confidence or expectation, possibly because of previous disappointments.

This model would suggest that many, if not most, adult students are actively seeking accreditation. Within the terms of this discussion, the group of adult students that is most 'problematic' (at least to colleges) is primarily located at quadrant C. Students in quadrants A and B are highly motivated towards achievement. Many students in quadrant D will be prompted to achieve by the external constraints being put upon them or may need access to something other than learning opportunities provided by a course or programme. This leaves quadrant C students. In order to draw some tentative conclusions about ways that colleges can raise achievement for students in this category, we need to revisit some issues around assessment.

Assessment revisited

One of the characteristics of teaching that promotes student achievement is the design and practice of assessment. The general features of good practice in assessment design (clarity of task, appropriateness and relevance, validity, sequencing, transparency of assessment criteria and the alignment of assessment with teaching and intended learning outcomes) are well known and have been discussed extensively elsewhere (Davis *et al.*, 1995). Two aspects that have received less attention within further and adult education are assessment and motivation, and assessment for learning.

Substantial development work has already taken place in higher education under the general heading of 'learning contracts' concerning the ways in which assessment can motivate students. In higher education this phase has a very different meaning from that usually given in further education. In universities, 'learning contracts' generally denote a process of discussion, negotiation and agreement of learning outcomes, learning tasks, resources, mutual commitments between student, tutor and university, and assessment content and format. The product of the process, the learning contract, can itself be used as a vehicle for assessment. Learning contracts have been used successfully in work-based learning, where managers and employers are looking for learning and assessment that are associated with solving real-time workplace problems (Robertson, 1992; Brennan and Little, 1996).

Such contracts are a radical departure from traditional higher education, and as a result require investment of time and energy to embed them into HE practice. Their outcomes suggest that the investment is worthwhile. They have achieved good success rates, widened access to higher education and substantially improved the engagement and motivation of students (and for that matter staff) (Brown and Baume, 1992; Stephenson and Laycock, 1993).

Assessment for learning

An authoritative survey of assessment recently concluded that one of the teaching strategies with the largest impact on student learning is formative assessment (Black and Wiliam, 1998). In some studies, formative assessment has a more positive effect on learning than on any other single factor, including prior learning (Scheerens and Bosker, 1997). To summarise a complex discussion, formative assessment stimulates the learning of all students and particularly low attaining students where:

- Students self-assess themselves at frequent intervals
- Grading is avoided in favour of the 'praise sandwich' (praise, instructions for improvement and praise again)
- Feedback is learner centred i.e. focused on the learner's achievement of assessment criteria, progress towards his/her personal target, praise for improvements and guidance on how further improvements can be made (Black and Wiliam, 1998).

It would seem that learning and assessment are not necessarily in conflict. Assessment can be highly motivating and can have a powerful and positive impact on student learning. Similar conclusions were drawn in an evaluation report (Astor, 1995) prepared for the Workers' Educational Association (WEA).

The links between assessment and learning in post-compulsory education have been established in a practical way by the WEA through its 'learning outcomes strategy'. The aim of the strategy is to find an acceptable way to demonstrate to students, tutors, funders and itself that worthwhile learning takes place in liberal studies courses. Early work is reported by Foster et al. (1997), and the practice has now been embedded throughout the WEA (WEA, 1998, 1999). Parallel work by the National Institute of Adult Continuing Education (NIACE) and the Oxfordshire Community Education Service demonstrates the huge range of possible assessment methods and tools to support self, peer, tutor and external assessment. In going back to first principles this work reinforces the importance of the links between assessment and learning (Donley and Napper, 1999). A synthesis of current developments is set out by Lavender (1999).

Objectors to the above arguments say that even if assessment can be motivating or can promote learning, it is frequently 'too bureaucratic', 'too time-consuming' or is generally 'too complicated'. These are serious criticisms, but they seem to be directed at technical issues rather than issues of principle. This type of technical problem seems largely to have been resolved within a number of flexible accreditation frameworks such as OCN accreditation, learning contracts and new and flexible qualifications based on similar principles and offered by the Scottish Qualifications Authority and English awarding bodies.

Raising adult achievement in practice

The achievements of adults have been raised by a variety of means within the colleges in this study. Specific attention has been paid to the problematic group of part-time adult learners (those with a high motivation to learn and a low motivation towards qualifications), mainly through the use of OCN accreditation.

One college has paid particular attention to adult modern languages students, partly because of the notorious problems of the mix of motivations, levels and attitudes towards assessment that can be found in many language classes (Lamping and Ball, 1996) – see Case Study 11.

Case Study 11. Department of Languages and Humanities, Oxford College of Further Education

Problem

- Mainly part-time modern language students: many did not want the existing LCCI accreditation.

Applied strategies

- Developed OCN accreditation for 14 languages over five levels
- Offered OCN units in addition to GCSEs and A-levels to allow for alternative, and partial, accreditation
- Achieved greater flexibility through developing a resource-based languages centre with a mixture of bought-in and self-developed resources that were based on OCN units.

Outcomes

- In 1996/7, 230 entries were made by 212 students who gained 460 credits.

Gloucestershire Adult and Continuing Education and Training (ACET) has developed a similar approach based around OCN accreditation across curriculum areas through a collaboration with colleges and other partners who deliver adult education under contract. It has:

- Developed an OCN credit framework for non-schedule 2 learning opportunities to encourage progression to schedule 2
- Encouraged providers to track all students
- Produced progression information sheets for tutors and students

- Rewarded the achievement of OCN credits through the contract with providers
- Underwritten students' OCN registration fees to help overcome any financial barriers
- Provided staff development opportunities for part-time tutors (many of whom teach for only one or two evenings a week) to promote shared values
- Established a peer inspection model using the Ofsted inspection framework; this involves a trained team of contract holder staff assessing teaching and learning at the point of delivery in organisations other than their own
- Set up a pilot project with the largest college to develop a peer observation model; this involves tutors being trained to observe sessions and give constructive feedback to their peers (the feedback is not graded).

Two further case studies illustrate improvements in retention and achievement among adults who have some ambivalence towards assessment and accreditation.

Case Study 12. Connections programme for adult returners at Norwich City College

Background

This programme was designed to widen the participation of adult students. Its special features included:

- A modular programme designed by experienced adult tutors and subject specialists
- Open Access
- Student-friendly 0930–1430 timetabling
- Significant tutorial support
- A variety of pick and mix, 30 hour modules.

Problem

Although the programme had been praised by external verifiers and inspectors, retention rates were not as good as had been anticipated. Research revealed that some enrollers never appeared, that some students felt ambivalent or hostile towards assessment and accreditation, and that the level of the programme was inappropriate for others.

Applied strategies

- There is a new managerial emphasis on retention to complement the earlier emphasis on widening participation.
- Work to explore and improve group dynamics has taken place.
- The design of assessment has been changed in order to make them less off-putting: from 'bite-sized' to 'straw-sized'.
- Basic skills modules have been introduced.

Outcomes

- Achievement rates increased by 8%
- New, pre-foundation modules were introduced with smaller groups and the support of classroom assistants
- Increased focus on inclusive learning approaches by staff
- A student liaison officer has been appointed and a greater emphasis is placed on tracking.

Case Study 13. Computing courses at Epping Forest College

Problems

- There were substantial differences in retention rates between different part-time courses.
- Around 10% of leavers left for largely external reasons.
- Among leavers, there were high levels of dissatisfaction concerning computing classes because students had joined a course of the wrong level or type.
- Some less experienced tutors were finding it difficult to cope with the diversity of students in their group and did not have sufficient information about other courses to advise students
- Problems relating to IT courses were particularly serious in that many adults were entering or re-entering formal learning through such courses.

Applied strategies

- Produced more informative prospectus and course leaflets
- Used initial (key skills diagnostic) test in first session
- Briefed all staff on the range of courses and arrangements for transfer
- Observed all new staff within first three weeks
- Introduced self-directed courses with learning materials and learning assistants as an alternative to classes.

Outcomes

In 1998, the withdrawal rate by mid November had been 13·7%.
At the same time in the following year, it had been reduced to 5%.

At the time of writing, the policy objectives of widening participation and lifelong learning seem to be somewhat at odds with other objectives in respect of audit, financial control and funding. On the one hand, the Government and the FEFC are committed to increasing take-up of education by adults. This is partly to achieve the objective of greater participation in formal education by hitherto under-represented groups (widening participation) and partly to encourage adults to engage in repeated, frequent and, if possible, continuous contact with education and development (lifelong learning). Means to achieve these objectives include:

- Additional funding for colleges
- Pilots to encourage colleges to recruit under-represented groups to innovative courses
- Pilots to fund college courses that are not assessed and accredited in the traditional way.

Colleges have responded enthusiastically to these objectives mainly through the development of relatively short programmes often at intermediate, entry or pre-entry level and accredited through OCN.

It is here that the tension in policy objectives becomes manifest. In England, the FEFC through its funding provision is also concerned to drive up standards, establish control procedures and ensure that it is securing value. This has led to a substantial tightening up of procedures around OCN-accredited programmes. Colleges have been told that OCN accreditation is not sufficient on its own to justify funding, but that they must also be able to demonstrate that students are progressing directly from OCN to courses accredited by other more conventional awarding bodies. Progression from entry to foundation level within OCN accredited provision, for example, will not suffice (FEFC, 1999d).

Despite the fact that the greatest demand from new adult learners is for programmes at the lowest level (pre-entry, entry and foundation), the pilots to fund non-accredited provision contain a requirement that students progress to accredited courses and that such courses are at Level 2 (FEFC, 1999a).

Until these tensions are resolved, arguments will continue between colleges and between funders, where the former will observe that the two sets of policy objectives are in conflict.

Key points

- Discussions about adult achievement are often polarised between those who see it as unproblematic and those who detect ambivalence, anxiety, lack of confidence or antagonism towards assessment and accreditation among adult students.
- Unless this issue can be resolved, it threatens to undermine the Government's policy to widen participation and promote lifelong learning.
- Analysis of the problem suggests that a particular focus of attention for colleges should be adult learners who may be relatively well motivated to learn but have little motivation to gain a qualification.
- Assessment techniques and accreditation frameworks have already been created which can provide student-friendly assessment opportunities.
- There is a growing body of quantitative research (mainly from the school sector) and action research (mainly from the adult and higher education sectors) that this type of student-centred assessment motivates students and promotes effective learning.
- There are currently tensions between policy objectives to widen participation and provide lifelong learning on the one hand and improve audit and financial control on the other. These tensions appear to be impacting on the development of programmes aimed at adults who are least highly motivated to achieve qualifications.

9 Support for achievement

Alongside changes to curriculum structure or approaches to teaching, colleges have been addressing issues relating to information, advice and guidance, placement on programmes, initial screening and testing, induction and diagnostic processes, arrangements for course transfer and student support. These issues are sometimes grouped under headings such as 'threshold', 'learner or student support' or 'student services'. The phrase that seems best to encompass them is 'support for achievement'. It has been argued that the effectiveness of this support is a key element in the success of strategies aimed at raising achievement (Martinez, 1999a).

These processes to support achievement are particularly under-researched in further education and there is little in the way of indicative research in the school or university sectors. FEDA is developing a research project in this area, but some generalisations can be made from the experiences of colleges reviewed here.

Most colleges pay close attention to the recruitment and selection aspects of this support. All colleges reviewed in this study have changed, developed and improved their practices in this area. Some of the measures taken are outlined below.

Information and advice

- Improving the way in which course requirements and demands are communicated to applicants (for example, Liverpool Community College)
- Providing pre-enrolment summer schools for arts subjects and basic skills (Canterbury College).

Entry criteria

- Putting greater emphasis on the selection of students against specified criteria (the music technology programme, Arnold and Carlton College)
- Tightening up exceptional entry procedures (Bridgwater College)
- Changing entry criteria (Humanities A-levels at Oxford College, Suffolk College, Huddersfield New College, the art and design programme at Barnsley College, Bury College, South Nottingham College)
- Curtailing late entry (West Kent College).

Interview and selection

- Making interview procedures more extensive or sophisticated (Humanities Faculty Oxford College, West Kent College)
- Having the interviews conducted by the most senior college managers: principal, vice-principals and assistant principals (Greenhead College)
- Having the interviews conducted by the person who is likely to be the student's personal tutor (Sparsholt College)
- Conducting second interviews in August to confirm the student's programme, learning agreement and learning support (Bridgwater College).

Initial screening and testing

- Introducing computer-assisted screening and
  diagnostic assessment (West Kent College)
- Liaising more closely with schools to obtain reports and
  references (Sutton Coldfield and Bridgwater colleges)
- Identifying at risk students very early on (Bridgwater, Luton Sixth Form,
  South Nottingham, Greenhead colleges and Humanities Faculty, Oxford College)
- Treating the first four to six weeks of the course as a diagnostic phase
  (Runshaw College, Humanities Faculty Oxford College)
- Running a 'check-your-choice' week at the end of October (Burnley College).

Course transfer

- Facilitating course change in the first weeks of term
  (Dewsbury and Bridgwater colleges)
- Encouraging students unsure of their A-level choice to begin four A-levels
  and to confirm their choice of three or four by half term (Greenhead College).

Many of the colleges that have tightened up their entry criteria were focusing on advanced level courses but Huddersfield New College and South Nottingham College, for example, introduced entry criteria for intermediate GNVQs (three or four GCSEs at grade D or above). Where these arrangements have been monitored, they seem to lead to a reduction in course transfers. At West Kent College, the percentage of A-level students changing one or more subjects declined from 16% (1996) to 5% (1998).

In parallel with efforts to improve the quality of selection and course placement, a number of colleges have also developed arrangements to build relationships with students between the offer of a place, and enrolment. Clearly, there are potential benefits in terms of the conversion of applications to enrolment, but these 'bonding' or 'relationship building' activities are also designed to aid in the preparation of students, in the communication of course and study requirements and in the formation of realistic expectations on the part of prospective students. Examples include:

- Inviting applicants to visit the college every
  six to eight weeks to meet course tutors and become
  familiar with their prospective course (East Birmingham College)
- Having contact between tutors and students immediately after students
  accept places (music technology at Arnold and Carlton College)
- Providing a comprehensive programme of tasters, open evenings,
  follow-up of individual students, more rapid administration, postcards and
  an advice service staffed throughout the summer (South Nottingham College)
- Moving the induction for full-time courses in June (Bridgwater College).

Strategies to inform, advise, guide and place students are sometimes driven centrally (often by heads of student services). South Nottingham College has a centrally driven strategy which is characterised by:

- Entry criteria being agreed for all levels of provision
  (e.g. four or more GCSEs at grade C or above for advanced programmes;
  four or more GCSEs at grade D or above for intermediate programmes)
- Quality control through random sampling of learning agreements
  (97–98% comply with these entry criteria)
- Clarity in all information and publicity material concerning entry
  criteria and course requirements
- The establishment of a central guidance team headed by a careers adviser and
  including staff with specific responsibilities for programmes at different levels

- All members of the guidance team working towards NVQ guidance qualifications at Level 3 and cascading their training to programme areas
- The use of on-course diagnostic assessments to supplement BSA tests
- 'Cause for concern' systems to identify at risk students to their personal tutors
- A scheme of work for induction and standardised materials and documentation produced to support induction activities
- College-wide procedures for students enrolling late (after the first week of term) including centrally delivered induction
- Agreement of criteria for progression from Year 1 to Year 2 of two-year courses
- Communication of progression requirements to students at the beginning of their programmes and use of such criteria to inform reviews of student progress, subsequently.

Bridgend College has also paid attention to the development of its central guidance services and these are reviewed in the case study below.

Case Study 14. Guidance Services at Bridgend College

Context
The college is in South Wales, located half way between Swansea and Cardiff, in an area that has been hard hit by industrial restructuring. It has 2000 full-time and 9000 part-time students and 500 staff, of whom slightly less than half are business support staff. Local schools have retained their sixth forms.

Problems
As at 1992:

- Underdeveloped guidance services
- Significant drop-out because students were often not vocationally focused and had unrealistic expectations of their programmes.

Applied strategies
Developed incrementally over a six-year period:

- All full-time students and 70% of part-time students are interviewed by departments; all applicants are offered guidance interviews prior to their departmental interview
- An adequately staffed and resourced guidance service was created that brought together marketing and guidance staff; the structure of the service is set out in Figure 16
- Regular staff training and encouragement of all front-line staff to achieve qualifications (NVQs 2/3 in Advice & Guidance)
- Involvement of admissions staff in the preparation of promotional literature and advertising to ensure that potential students are offered a realistic and accurate picture of the college
- Partnerships including regular liaison with careers teachers and the local careers service, maintaining school-college link programmes, providing information events for employers, participating in the local adult guidance network and the schools-industry forum
- Students can only transfer from one course to another following an interview with the guidance adviser
- In order to extend the range of services available, the guidance service tenders for and delivers cost recovery work for the local TEC, Employment Services and local education authority (currently generating £400k annual income).

Figure 16. Organisational chart for admissions and guidance/training office

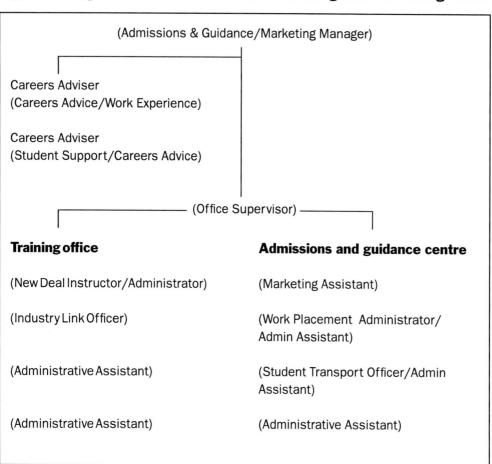

(Admissions & Guidance/Marketing Manager)

Careers Adviser
(Careers Advice/Work Experience)

Careers Adviser
(Student Support/Careers Advice)

(Office Supervisor)

Training office

(New Deal Instructor/Administrator)

(Industry Link Officer)

(Administrative Assistant)

(Administrative Assistant)

Admissions and guidance centre

(Marketing Assistant)

(Work Placement Administrator/
Admin Assistant)

(Student Transport Officer/Admin
Assistant)

(Administrative Assistant)

Outcomes

- Some 1500 students take up the offer of an additional guidance interview each year.
- Significant improvement in relationships with schools: college guidance staff are invited to schools and a number of GNVQ, GCSE and key skills programmes are being shared between college and schools.

It is clear that threshold activities make an important impact on achievement and retention and that their success depends on an effective relationship and partnership between central specialist staff and curriculum teams. Colleges have therefore made efforts to improve and integrate the activities of staff involved in:

- Advice and guidance
- Interviewing and selection
- Initial testing and induction.

Walsall College of Arts & Technology has been developing its threshold procedures with a particular focus on adult students for several years. The college has now replaced its earlier Activate programmes (reviewed in Martinez, 1996) with a more comprehensive STAR programme. This aims to widen participation by providing accredited, customised pathways into employment for non-traditional students, the long-term unemployed and disadvantaged adults. The pathways include elements of guidance, counselling, confidence building, skills development, work trialling, training and work experience, job-search assistance and direct support while in employment. The initial diagnostic phase comprises an interview and initial assessment. The second stage has three different pathways depending on the outcomes of the diagnostic phase. Broadly, students who do not need much support will progress to a Fast Track in one of the 10 vocational areas provided by the college. Students who need to access ongoing support in terms of guidance, basic or study skills, join an Assisted Fast Track programme. Students who need most support to achieve their goals join the Full Support Track. The three tracks are represented in Figure 17.

Figure 17. Walsall STAR Programme

Fast Track	Assisted Fast Track	Full Support Track
Initial diagnostic interview	Initial diagnostic interview	Initial diagnostic interview
Initial assessment	Initial assessment	Initial assessment
Into vocational areas	Vocational training NVQ/GNVQ with qualifications	Vocational tasters – with qualifications (possible Discrete Programme – or Infill)
Possible discrete programmes (depending on numbers)	Emphasis on stand alone key skills through vocational training	Skill power
Programme/NVQ/ GNVQ starts April/June–December (No summer break)	Programme starts April/June	Emphasis on stand alone key skills through vocational tasters
Under 16 hours – or link to full-time work skills	Ongoing vocational guidance	Key skills include literacy, numeracy, communication, ESOL, basic IT skills, job search, confidence building, inter-personal skills
Ongoing vocational guidance and key skills	Job search	Programme starts April/June
Job search	Personal development/ improve job prospects	Ongoing vocational guidance
Personal development/ improve job prospects		Job search
		Personal development/improve job prospects

The STAR programme was developed in partnership with the College of Continuing Education (Walsall), the Employment Service regional manager and the local employment service business manager. To create the programme three days of initial staff development were then followed up by further staff development, the appointment of specialised tutoring staff (an entry level tutor and an ESOL tutor) and the production of a tutor guide and handbook.

Initial interviews are conducted in job centres; more specialist interviews are carried out in college. Students retain links with the same staff who interviewed and inducted them on to one of the Tracks. On the Fast or Assisted Fast Track, if students are unsure about their vocational goals, they can join the four-week taster programme with the intention of trying out three or four vocational programmes and starting to develop their key skills. The STAR programme runs all year round and has provided a ready vehicle for New Deal students.

At the end of the pilot period 95% of the first group of 808 STAR programme participants completed or were continuing with their programme. Of completers, more than 80% had achieved their qualification aim.

Finally, the case of Hairdressing and Beauty Therapy at North Warwickshire and Hinckley College illustrates some of the difficulties and subtleties of giving information and placing students on the relevant course. Staff concluded that a significant reason for drop-out was that some students were neither adequately prepared for, nor had a realistic understanding of, their course. The department decided to:

- Make special interview arrangements for all students who put down only 'hairdressing' or 'beauty therapy' on their application form
- Interview such students by a panel which brought together teachers from different courses to advise and guide as well as select
- Require applicants for more specialised part-time courses (where problems had occurred in the past) to attend information and interview events
- Coordinate this activity by identifying a tutor with lead responsibilities for admissions.

These changes were part of a strategy developed in the department to improve retention and achievement. (See case study in Appendix 3.)

Student services

It might seem odd to have a section on Student Services in a guide focused mainly on achievement, rather than retention. There are five reasons for this:

- In a number of colleges, Student Services has a significant role in developing and sometimes leading strategies to improve achievement and retention.
- A college perspective that takes an overview of student progress is often associated with Student Services, particularly in FE and tertiary colleges.
- Even where they do not have direct control, Student Services managers seem often to exercise considerable influence over key aspects of students' learning experiences.
- A variable mix of student support and sometimes learning support services tends to be located within Student Services.
- In the words of one head of Student Services, 'in a college, students have their most intimate relationships with teachers, but outside the experience of teaching and learning, Student Services often is the college' (Joslin, 1999).

The role of Student Services varies considerably from college to college. While colleges tend to deliver broadly the same mix of services, the boundaries between Student Services, curriculum managers and sometimes resource managers are drawn quite differently. Insofar as common themes can be identified, Student Services seem to:

- Be responsible for delivering support to students via a mixture of counselling, welfare, information and advice, childcare and financial support services
- Influence the design, delivery, documentation and standards of tutoring, even though the line management of tutors usually falls within curriculum areas (Harrogate, Runshaw, Liverpool, Canterbury, Reading and Bridgwater Colleges)
- Lead college-based research on student drop-out or on the reasons that applications do not lead to enrolments (Canterbury, Harrogate); this might include research conducted through exit or early leaver interviews
- Be entrusted with management of continuing careers education and guidance processes usually included in the accreditation of job search or career skills development (Basford Hall, Harrogate, East Birmingham Colleges)
- Be involved in student tracking, attendance monitoring and the follow up of non-authorised absence (Runshaw, Regent, Luton Sixth Form Colleges)
- Share in developing health, sports and curriculum enrichment activities (Harrogate).

Key points

- Support for achievement encompasses all those processes that help to place and support students on programmes of study: information, advice, guidance, recruitment and selection, careers education, initial screening and testing, induction, arrangements for course transfer and student support for achievement.
- The case studies in preceding chapters on teaching and curriculum strategy usually include changes to the management of this support.
- The colleges included in the research have changed, developed and improved their threshold procedures to ensure that students are appropriately placed on courses.
- The range of strategies extends from initial information and advice through interviews and relationship building prior to enrolment, to induction, extended diagnostic testing and course transfer arrangements.
- Some colleges have blurred the distinction between guidance, taster, induction and diagnostic processes through the introduction of freestanding modules leading to alternative programmes.
- Student Services functions often play a key role in the design, development and implementation of strategies aimed at improving student achievement.

10 | Staff motivation

I f students need motivating, so do staff. Recently published research suggested that much of the energy and time available for teacher development was taken up with maintenance activities (coping with curriculum change, new syllabi, new assessment requirements and so on) rather than being focused on improvements in student retention and achievement (Martinez, 1999b). Other recent studies have explored reasons for a growing volume of complaints about bureaucracy and red tape in colleges (Martinez and Pepler, 1999). Problems of morale and motivation among teachers in the years since incorporation have also been highlighted (Taubman *et al.*, 1998; Warren, 1998; Yarrow and Esland, 1998; Robson, 1998). An accessible overview of staff motivation in relation to school effectiveness and improvement is contained in Visscher (1999).

The overwhelming message from school effectiveness and school improvement research is that teachers are central to all efforts to improve achievement, something which the experience of colleges reviewed above amply demonstrates. It is not surprising, therefore, that motivating staff is an integral part of strategies designed to raise achievement. The five main ways in which this is done is via:

- Team development
- Information and awareness raising
- Continuing professional development through action research and mentoring
- Efforts to reduce bureaucracy
- A shared approach to the management of change.

Team development

Team development approaches can be subdivided into those that:

- Focus exclusively on team teaching, the development of an appropriate mix of team skills and improvements in the coordination of teaching and assessment
- Seek to combine the first set of pedagogic issues with the devolution of budget and decision-making responsibilities.

Most colleges are somewhere on a spectrum between the two extremes and commonly combine the professional development approach with some managerial responsibilities.

Fairly 'pure' examples of the pedagogic approach can be found at Sutton Coldfield College, Solihull College, Solihull Sixth Form College and Arnold and Carlton College. Sutton Coldfield College has allocated two hours of regular weekly slots for course team meetings and development. Team meetings have standing agenda items on student progress and performance and the college has provided staff development and management support to ensure that meetings are action oriented. Teams provide the natural focus for efforts to improve delivery, and seek continuous improvements.

In the other colleges, teaching groups are engaged in:

- Collaborative and shared development of new teaching strategies and course materials (History Department at Solihull Sixth Form College)
- The implementation of team teaching (Music Technology at Arnold and Carlton College)
- Providing a unitised curriculum and developing abilities to teach across a number of teacher education courses (Solihull College)
- Adopting the principle that all members of the (small) team teach on all modules (Advanced Leisure and Tourism team at Lowestoft College)
- Ad hoc teams, including students (Harrogate).

A case study from Travel and Tourism at West Herts College illustrates this approach.

Case Study 15. Travel and Tourism at West Herts College

Problems: 1995/96

- Good recruitment but poor retention among advanced students
- Poor recruitment and poor achievement among intermediate students
- High staff turnover
- Block work placements in Spring term
- Late changes to educational visits
- Irregular team meetings
- Patchy implementation of decisions.

Applied strategies

- Clarified course and year tutor roles
- Improved and made uniform the administrative and tracking system
- Introduced a more stable teaching team
- Held regular team meetings and improved team working
- Established three pathways for different career goals each with different additional studies (air cabin crew, travel operations, tour guides/representatives)
- Moved block work placement to end of year
- Provided different additional units
- Planned educational visits well in advance
- Restructured programme to provide opportunities for mid-year unit achievement.

Outcomes

Figure 18. Retention, progression and achievement rates for Travel and Tourism at West Herts College 1997/98

	Intermediate	Advanced	
		Year 1	Year 2
Retention (%)	78	86	97
Progression (%)	—	100	—
Achievement (%)	74	—	97

In 1998/99 the improving trend on both intermediate and advanced programmes continues, although the rate of improvement is less dramatic. There has been a further large increase in advanced student enrolments.

Approaches which combine the pedagogic and professional development of teams with the devolution of managerial roles can be found at Great Yarmouth and Canterbury Colleges.

Great Yarmouth has adopted the principle of self-managing teams. Essentially, the 12 teams:

- Elect their own team leader
- Retain 60% of the income generated by their activity
- Are responsible for delivering this activity to target and taking remedial action if required
- Determine the availability of remission to team members
- Retain a proportion of any surplus of income over target.

Teams at Canterbury have devolved budgets and can carry forward surpluses (or deficits) to the next academic and financial year.

Information and awareness raising

Teachers may be pessimistic about improving the achievement of their students where student outcomes have been poor for some time or have deteriorated even though teaching and assessment strategies have stayed roughly the same. Low expectations may also be associated with subjects which have poor achievement nationally.

One of the common elements of staff development programmes to raise student achievement is information and awareness raising (Martinez *et al.*, 1997). The aims of information strategies are usually to share or communicate:

- Research which helps to clarify the nature of retention/achievement problems
- Research conducted within the college
- Experience of successful interventions to improve retention/achievement within the college
- Information about strategies that have been successful in other colleges
- College plans to improve achievement and retention.

This type of information and communication strategy is occasionally supported by newsletters or intranet newsletters. For example, Barking College has developed a lively newsletter to share tips and ideas, challenge myths and raise awareness. The front page of the first issue is reproduced in Figure 19.

Figure 19. Barking College internal newsletter

Improving Retention – Good Ideas Sheet 1

Some ideas from the Retention
Task Group for improving the retention of students

There is no one answer to retaining students but there is a target of 82% retention on all courses. The Retention Task group have identified several reasons why students leave the course unfinished. A number of ideas for improving retention are listed below. Many of them you may have tried before. None of them are the complete answer, so you may have to try several. If you want to talk to one of us we would be happy to discuss these ideas and would welcome any other suggestions. A list of members is set out at the end of the sheet. It is hoped that this will be the first of several ideas sheets.

Reasons for leaving

1. Financial -

*"I can't afford
.... the fees
the costs of travelling
childcare
textbooks
equipment.........."*

So what can you do?

- Don't let the fees come as a surprise - give details in all course literature including an indication of the costs of registration or assessment fee. Remember to put in the fees for both under 19 and over 19

- Offer the help of the College Counsellor - Sue Kemmis (ext.2265) she cannot work miracles but does have some money in a hardship fund, information on trusts which might help and can advise on social benefit rights

- Let all students know if they have to buy textbooks. Try to have some on short term loan by the library, talk to the Students Union about their new second hand book service. Talk to Iris Lewis (ext 2259) or Caroline Ledward (ext 2287) for details

- Advertise and encourage students to use the discount software service

Continuing professional development

The most widespread form of continuing professional development to improve achievement is action research. This seems to be quite different from the main forms of staff development for student retention where action research was present in only a handful of colleges (Martinez *et al.*, 1998). There are four possible explanations for this:

- The sector has matured quite rapidly since the earlier work on retention
- Achievement is arguably more complex and problematic than retention; colleges may feel that they need to situate their strategies more securely within a research tradition
- Achievement issues are intimately bound up with pedagogy and there is a developed tradition of action research connected with classroom practice
- The more colleges focus their efforts on improving student outcomes, the more sophisticated their approaches have become and, it would seem, their current improvement methods tend to take the form of action research.

Cohen and Manion (1994) provide a convenient definition of this approach:

> [action research] *is essentially on-the-spot procedure designed to deal with a concrete problem located in an immediate situation. This means that ideally, the step-by-step process is constantly monitored over varying periods of time and by a variety of mechanisms (questionnaires, diaries, interviews and case studies, for example) so that the ensuing feedback may be translated into modifications, adjustments, directional changes, redefinitions as necessary, so as to bring about lasting benefit to the ongoing process itself rather than to some future occasion, as is the purpose of more traditionally oriented research. Unlike other methods, no attempt is made to identify one particular factor and study it in isolation, divorced from the context giving it meaning.*

Two case studies illustrate the type of action research approach being adopted. Uxbridge College used a literature search to start the development of its strategy for GNVQ foundation students. In the absence of significant work in the tertiary sector in Britain, the college looked at relevant work done in schools and in community colleges in the United States. It also used interviews, analysis of registers and student surveys of foundation level students and of students on similar programmes within the college. The outcomes informed the curriculum restructure and the teaching and learning strategies reviewed above on pp55.

The college used a range of ways to monitor and then adjust the implementation of this strategy including:

- Student questionnaires
- Tutorials and regular assessments to monitor progress
- Staff meetings to monitor student performance/progress
- Focus groups to allow students to provide feedback to the college (a specific focus group on attendance issues was part of the research into the effectiveness of the learning coordinators)
- Monthly senior management team meetings and course team meetings to monitor retention
- Research into student attendance, attitudes to attendance and strategies for improvement
- Participation in events and conferences organised by FEDA and others to provide comparisons with other colleges.

The careful ways in which the initiative was monitored and evaluated has contributed to its success and provided a basis to extend some aspects of the strategy to other parts of the curriculum.

A similar process was adopted at Liverpool Community College: a research phase followed by the selection of strategies, ongoing monitoring and formative evaluation, and the periodic adjustment of priorities. The initial phase included an information search through participation in FEDA conferences; exchanging ideas and information with a neighbouring college (Knowsley), the creation of a Retention Strategy Group, participation in the *9000 voices* research (Martinez and Munday, 1998) to investigate retention issues in the college, and analysis of the college's own data.

During the preparatory phase the college undertook some additional research on tutoring in order to:

- Investigate the operation of the tutorial system
- Assess the effectiveness of tutorials
- Gather student opinion
- Assess the quality of recording documentation
- Identify good practice.

A summary of the outcomes of the retention and tutoring research was made available within the college.

Two main initiatives were developed as outcomes of the research and preparatory phases: a college interventionist project (reviewed in the next chapter) and a tutorial development programme. In both cases, activities were supported by information and awareness raising seminars, staff development events, internal consultancy, training customised to the needs of particular teams and curriculum areas, the provision of guides, checklists and learning materials, and a staff bulletin. As in Uxbridge, particular attention was paid to formative evaluation and periodic reporting with an additional focus on disseminating information widely within a large college (Liverpool Community College Courier, 1997).

The way in which colleges in this survey have linked staff development and action through action research has inspired the current FEDA programme of development projects to raise achievement and improve retention.

Observation and mentoring

Two other forms of staff development that are being used quite extensively are observation and mentoring. Many of the colleges in the survey have extended their teacher observation systems to include tutoring and part-time staff (for example, at South Nottingham College). Sometimes the purpose has been narrowly defined as observation for self-assessment purposes, conducted by managers or a select observation team. More usually the process has an explicit professional development objective including peers or a wider group of observers.

Substantial benefits are being reported in terms of the dissemination of good practice, an increase in professional discussions and exchanges and the widening and renewal of teaching strategies among both observers and observees. Similar effects have been identified by the FEFC (1999b). Some colleges have emphasised the importance of openness, professional exchange and feedback by including principals and other senior managers in the observation and feedback process.

Mentoring is inspired by a desire to increase professional exchanges between teachers. Until now, it has largely been employed in the induction of and support for newly recruited or promoted members of staff. In a number of colleges in this report, it has been used to provide focused support and development for continuous improvement purposes. Examples include:

- Mentoring linked to twice yearly teacher observation (South Nottingham College)
- Senior management team 'buddies' who mentor programme leaders (East Birmingham College).

In Llandrillo College, the mentoring scheme provides a core element of the college's strategy to improve retention and achievement and is reviewed in the following case study.

Case Study 16. Mentoring at Llandrillo College

Context

Llandrillo is a large college based in Colwyn Bay, North Wales (24 000 enrolments) on four sites and with numerous outreach centres.

Problems

- Some course teams tended to see retention and achievement as management problems
- Existing good practice was not being shared
- Responses to perceived retention and achievement issues tended to focus exclusively on stiffening entry criteria.

Applied strategies

Introduced a Teaching and Learning Mentor Scheme whose aims are to:

- Help course teams to identify and address issues and disseminate good practice
- Provide a focus on solutions rather than a blame culture
- Contribute to self-assessment
- Give ownership to course teams who decide how and when mentoring takes place.

Implementation of the mentoring scheme involved:

- Allocating one mentor to all 22 programme areas, trained by one of Her Majesty's Inspectors (HMI)
- Setting trigger levels for performance indicators, which are approved by the relevant head of school and reviewed twice yearly: the upper levels trigger dissemination; the lower levels trigger action
- Designating as performance indicators student feedback, attendance, retention and achievement
- The mentor and team:
  - Discussing and exploring how and why the trigger has been activated
  - Developing a course of action (e.g. classroom observation, staff development, dissemination of good practice etc.)

- Stipulating that contact with mentors can be initiated by the head of school or programme area manager or by teachers directly
- Mentors meeting with the college quality manager on a monthly basis mainly to share good practice between programme areas.

An example of a set of triggers agreed for a specific course is shown in Figure 20. SPOPs refer to the student perception of programme evaluations.

Figure 20. Llandrillo College: Teaching and Learning Mentor Scheme example of triggers

Programme area:

Course:

Date agreed:

Course Coordinator:

Performance indicator	Lower trigger (Warning signal)	Reasons	Upper trigger (Level for dissemination of good practice)	Reasons
Attendance	Below 75%	Unlikely to achieve if below this figure	95%	Past records show attendance is always below 95%
Retention	65%	National comparators 65% Past retention rates 64%	80%	Would be an achievement on this particular course
Attainment	90% of completers	Always been 95–100% in the past	100% of completers	
SPOPS	Below 70% 'very good to excellent' for teaching and learning	Past SPOPs above this	90–100% 'very good to excellent' for teaching and learning	

HoS signature:

> **Outcomes**
>
> - Teaching teams have become much more 'hungry' for data.
> - Student evaluations of the college have improved.
> - Course teams are more focused on pedagogic and curriculum issues and student outcomes.
> - The process of setting triggers has been refined: initially, some were set so high (or low) that they could never be activated.
> - A number of changes to both teaching course structure have occurred ranging from timetabled length of sessions (Leisure and Tourism, National Diploma) to the introduction of team teaching, to improved cover arrangements, to more varied teaching strategies (GNVQ Business Advanced).
> - Improvements in retention, attendance and achievement have been noted but the absence of reliable historical data makes comparisons difficult.

Efforts to reduce bureaucracy

To summarise briefly some parallel FEDA research:

- Bureaucracy and red tape are making significant and growing demands on lecturer time.
- The growth in bureaucratic burdens is being driven from within colleges and is mainly associated directly with students or with the administration of teaching and learning.
- These types of administrative requirements are likely to grow in the foreseeable future.
- Some colleges have made significant progress in mitigating or reducing bureaucratic burdens.
- The type of steps colleges have taken include: applying business process; reengineering principles to administrative systems; reviewing administrative tasks and devolving some of them to support staff; simplifying and streamlining administrative procedures; applying new technology and 'gatekeeping' activities by senior managers (Martinez and Pepler, 1999).

Several of the colleges in this study were also included in the parallel research on reducing bureaucracy. The two processes appear to go hand in hand and it seems that staff motivation is the theme that links the two together. Examples of strategies to reduce bureaucracy include:

- Developing in-house management information system (MIS) software which produces comprehensive reports for individual courses on a single side of A4, and on-line (Huddersfield New College)
- Senior managers adopting a conscious strategy to reduce unnecessary meetings and to limit or constrain administrative demands emanating from outside the college (Greenhead College)
- Redesigning support staff roles to ensure that valuable tutoring time is not consumed by data gathering activities (Hartlepool College)
- Using ICT to generate target minimum grades and record student progress in ways that can be accessed by subject and personal tutors (Luton Sixth Form and Winstanley colleges)
- Reducing and simplifying GNVQ paperwork (Sutton Coldfield and Runshaw colleges)
- Streamlining the administration of learning support (Bridgwater College)
- Using fully computerised attendance recording (Luton Sixth Form, Huddersfield New and Regent colleges)

- Adopting common documentation across the college
  (East Birmingham College)
- Standardising formats for GNVQ paperwork
  (Sutton Coldfield, Runshaw and Huddersfield New colleges)
- Inputting registers into an electronic format by clerical assistants
  (Sutton Coldfield College) or through an optical mark reader (OMR)
  scanner (West Kent College, Liverpool Community College).

Management of change

Finally, a number of colleges have sought to engage and motivate staff through the processes by which raising achievement strategies have been developed and implemented. These are discussed in the next chapter.

Key points

- Staff motivation is a key element in strategies to improve achievement.
- The main strategies to motivate staff seem to be: team development; information and awareness raising; continuing professional development; efforts to reduce bureaucracy; a shared approach to the management of change.
- Considerable attention is being given to develop effective teaching teams and, to a lesser extent, devolve managerial responsibility to such teams.
- Information and awareness raising strategies have been used to share good practice from within and outside a college and to challenge untested assumptions about student achievement.
- Continuing professional development is important – partly for its own sake and partly to motivate staff.
- In this context the most prevalent forms of continuing professional development include action research, the observation of teaching and learning and mentoring.
- Many colleges are also attempting to motivate staff by reducing bureaucracy and red tape.

11

Processes for raising achievement

S trategies used by colleges to improve retention are very diverse. In some colleges, change is being led by senior managers; in others by department heads or course teams. Some strategies are college wide; others are located in individual programme areas or courses. Ad hoc task groups and campaigns are created alongside the normal quality and line management systems in some colleges; in others, strategies are being driven and developed through strategic and operational planning, review and quality assurance mechanisms.

The originators of change involved in raising achievement are similarly diverse, ranging from principals and other senior managers to heads of department or faculty, course teams and individual teachers, heads of student services, and managers with quality assurance responsibilities. Examples of all can be found in the case studies included in this guide. Similarly, a variety of approaches are being used either to work alongside, through or transform college planning and review and quality mechanisms.

This said, many of the colleges in this study used processes that differ from those described in *Improving student retention* (Martinez, 1997). They are distinguished by their:

- Inclusivity and shared approach
- Developmental nature
- Mixture of elements of 'control' and 'empowerment'
- Foundation in research.

Inclusivity and shared approach

Where achievement strategies are based on the collaborative work of course or programme teams, inclusivity is not particularly an issue. Where colleges – and particularly large colleges – are seeking improvements in achievement across a number of curriculum areas, they frequently create task or implementation or support groups to:

- Provide channels of communication
- Develop and improve their strategies
- Share effective practice
- Share ownership
- Secure commitment.

It does not seem coincidental that the most fully articulated strategy to include staff was developed at Liverpool Community College, the largest college included in this research. This cross-college strategy revolves around action research and targeted interventions, coordinated by a cross-college Retention Strategy Group and a

Retention Working Group. The milestones in the development of this inclusive process are set out in Figure 21.

Figure 21. Liverpool Community College: strategies to improve retention and achievement

---

1997–98

- Responsibilities for the coordination and development of retention strategies were allocated to a college manager.
- Retention Strategy Group was established, chaired by a member of the senior management team.
- Awareness raising events were led by the senior management team for middle managers and, then cascaded by middle managers for course teams.
- The college undertook research within the *9000 voices* FEDA project.
- Interventionist project work commenced in nine courses.
- Regular reports were produced for the Academic Board.
- Retention issues were reviewed course by course.
- A Retention Working Group was created to oversee and support the interventionist project.

1998–99

- A register monitoring exercise was conducted for 100 courses.
- The tutoring development initiative was begun.
- The Retention Working Group conducted a course evaluation.
- All teams were encouraged to develop local initiatives to improve retention.
- A cross-college retention strategy was developed.
- Programme area managers were asked to produce their local strategies and present them to a meeting of senior managers.
- Targeted intervention strategies were extended to 19 courses.
- A checklist for managers was created, the first item of which requires them to: involve the whole of their course team in setting retention targets; collectively discuss ways to improve retention; and regularly monitor retention levels using MIS data. A copy of the checklist is given in Appendix 5·1.

Outcomes

- Improvement strategies are being developed and implemented throughout the college.
- There has been a 9% improvement in retention rates across all courses over the three-year period.

While somewhat smaller in scale, similar working parties or task groups were established at:

- Barking College: retention task group to conduct research, develop strategies, support their implementation and initiate action research projects
- Reading College of Technology and School of Art: focus group to review and improve tutoring
- Canterbury and Harrogate Colleges: cross-college working parties led by the heads of Student Services
- Telford College: working parties to plan the implementation of the new curriculum structure.

Developmental nature of strategies

The strategies that are reviewed below are those that are developed and implemented within an explicit action research framework (see previous chapter) and evolve over time as colleges learn incrementally from their own experience and that of others.

The first example is Lewes Tertiary College, which was set up in 1989 through a merger of three school sixth forms. Its strategies were developed over a two-year period to improve outcomes particularly in respect of its advanced level programmes. In the first year (1995–96) the deputy principal (for curriculum) conducted interviews with each A-level course team to look at items related to:

- Entry: selection, provision of information, preparedness of students
- On programme: teaching/learning process/style, syllabus, resources, learning materials, pace, revision/monitoring/learning support
- End of course: previous results, targets for each programme area and action planning.

The deputy principal then produced a report on the whole A-level programme, which identified good practice and problems and then made recommendations.

In the second and following years, the programme managers responsible for A-level programmes (across the college), GNVQ and later GCSE took over leadership of the process and:

- Followed up subjects that were not meeting targets
- Set year-on-year improvement targets
- Identified and publicised good and poor practice
- Challenged complacency and required an explanation of poor results
- Revised the curriculum offer and dropped some subjects
- Revisited priorities periodically (for example the priority has currently shifted away from A–E passes at A-level towards A–C).

The outcomes of this approach include:

- An increase in average A-level point scores from 10·9 to 14·9
- Year-on-year increases in:
  o A–E A-level passes to 89%
  o GNVQ passes to 82%.

After the general framework had been created, implementation of the strategy was devolved to middle managers. A similar process of 'drilling down' can be identified at Barnfield College (see above pp26). At Runshaw College, by contrast, the development has taken the form of a series of interlinked strategies which have evolved over time.

In 1996–97, Runshaw College launched its 'New beginnings' strategy. This identified that the major issue for the college was to renew its emphasis on quality and on student discipline and behaviour. In the following year, the strategy was 'Raising achievement', focusing on the introduction of target minimum grades for all full-time students. This was succeeded by 'High expectations' (1998–99), which focused on student perceptions of themselves and their aspirations. The setting of target minimum grades was extended to all students and measures were developed to support this, such as directed study.

Developmental strategies are also characterised by the abandonment or adjustment of strategies that do not work as well as those that do. In the context of some highly successful interventions and innovations, Regent College saw that some measures did not work as well as anticipated, notably induction for new enrolments and making lead tutors responsible for agreeing changes to student learning agreements. West Kent College found that centralising initial diagnostic assessment did not work as smoothly as planned, largely because many tutors felt excluded by the new procedures. This aspect of the college's strategy has evolved and now initial assessment is administered by personal tutors, who give immediate and sympathetic feedback to students. The centralisation of all diagnostic testing at Bridgwater was abandoned, mainly for logistical reasons, in favour of a devolved process supervised by the head of learner services.

The most marked example of a process which changed and developed over time is provided by Burnley College. Retention and achievement have been major college priorities for three years. The first year could be characterised as a 'control phase'. This was centrally led, focused on outcomes and formulated issues almost exclusively around 'problem courses' which were more than 20% below a college-wide target for retention. Procedures were tightened up, policies were introduced or rewritten, one course was closed and interview procedures were standardised in this first year. Average retention rates increased by about 3% but the college felt that it would be difficult to secure further improvements unless the process was changed.

In the second year, a more supportive and exploratory strategy was developed. Deficiencies in data-collecting and recording were recognised and addressed. Course teams were encouraged to consider their own performance and to produce evaluations based on evidence from the newly recruited student representatives at course team meetings, student surveys, student focus group discussions, 'mystery customers' and the course team's own attendance, retention and achievement data. Parents of students under 19 were introduced to tutors, provided with copies of course outlines and timetables and invited to attend any disciplinary meeting involving their children. However, these changes were essentially centrally driven, as were changes to college induction guidelines.

In the third year, the emphasis became more developmental, focusing on devolution and experimentation. Course teams were encouraged to move from centrally determined strategies in favour of developing their own. In taking this step, senior managers were acknowledging that different issues were at play in different courses and that strategies might need to change on the same course from one year to the next. This general approach was supported by several classroom-based action research projects:

- Investigating excellence in teaching and learning
- Doubling the amount of tutoring time for full-time students
- Developing target minimum grades for A-levels
- Introducing vivas, new assignments and progress reporting for art and design students
- Developing an enhancement programme with the local careers service for students most at risk of dropping out
- Organising meetings between tutors and the parents of all younger full-time students.

The outcomes have been very encouraging. 'Start-to-finish' retention rates have increased from 63% to 80% (for two-year programmes) and from 65% to 78% (for one-year programmes) over a three-year period (1995–98).

Control and empowerment

Three generalisations that emerge from the management of change literature are that: there are very few hard and fast rules; there is generally a trade-off between rapid implementation (typically associated with top-down approaches) and capacity building and organisational learning (usually associated with more participative approaches); change strategies are by necessity highly context specific i.e. what will be successful in one context may fail in another.

Further patterns emerge from the present research:

- Most colleges are adopting a mixture of top-down and shared or bottom-up approaches.

- Highly prescriptive approaches are generally associated with data collection procedures.
- The uses and interpretation of such data are generally characterised by a shared or even bottom-up approach.
- Target-setting is increasingly being devolved to teams but may be moderated or agreed with senior managers.
- The implementation of strategies to achieve targets is largely left to programme teams and individual teachers.
- Many colleges have also developed significant centrally driven strategies such as the introduction of target minimum grades or the redesign of their tutorial systems; these are often planned and implemented with the help of a task or project group.

The ways in which colleges manage information through a mixture of top-down and shared approaches illustrates these points well. Much has been made in recent months of the continuing difficulties some colleges have in providing data to funding and inspection authorities (FEFC, 1999c). Deficiencies in data collection and data management are particularly serious for college management at all levels from teacher to principal (Martinez and Munday, 1998). One of the most comprehensive strategies to improve the management of information has been developed at South East Essex College. The cornerstone of strategies to increase effectiveness at the college has been a continuous and significant effort to improve the collection and management of information. This has:

- Ensured that the college can be managed efficiently as a business
- Informed the development and implementation of curriculum strategies
- Provided information to external stakeholders
- Underpinned performance management including teachers' management of their own performance.

This last point is worth repeating. Course tutors need access to information that enables them to make realistic assessments of their performance. Such information needs to be 'transparent and accessible and provide the opportunity for every teacher to be pleased, celebrated or embarrassed' (Pitcher, 1998). Investment in systems and managerial time has enabled the college to produce and circulate accurate and detailed information on a course-by-course basis, three times a year. The third annual report (e.g. South East Essex College, 1998) contains information on:

- Total enrolments
- Enrolment at each of three census dates
- All withdrawals from enrolments to the third census date
- Retention rates as a percentage of enrolments to the third census date.

Aspects of the management of teaching which are underpinned by this information include:

- Rigorous benchmarking against other colleges and schools
- Target-setting and review
- Public praise and celebration of achievement
- Questioning and challenging of assertions that can not be evidenced
- Promotion of professional discussions and peer support
- Close, supportive management of teaching
- Clear, demonstrable, disappointment in poor performance
- An action and improvement orientation (Pitcher, 1998).

Greenhead and East Birmingham colleges, while very different from each other, have both adopted similar strategies for broadly similar reasons.

The information gathering system at Greenhead College is based on value added analysis. The benefits of the system are referred to above, and have been summarised as follows:

This has been powerful in allowing us as a staff to identity areas of strengths and weaknesses to work on by cross-college discussions in staff groups using (summative value added results) as a stimulus. Each staff member and department can draw forth useful conclusions for continuing improvement, by analysing why other departments, or colleagues can manage to achieve better outcomes with the same students. This has been excellent in-service training. (Conway, 1997)

The general intention is to create a 'researching college' through processes that empower teachers. The task of senior managers is to create a college where 'everyone is an individual, everyone is an exception, everyone is valuable – students and teachers' (ibid).

The value added system at Greenhead is now sufficiently mature that teachers expect to receive their own value added analysis and relevant comparator information. Staff development days are devoted to reviewing and analysing the data, at first across the college, then in departmental groups to generate commentaries and subsequently action plans. The process has inspired a number of teaching innovations, notably: the development of resource bases, the introduction of a 'circus of experiments' in physics and enhancement lessons at lunchtime and in the late afternoon for some subjects. As to control, the system is centrally led. Where departments are unable to resolve problems internally, senior managers have intervened to bring in a chief examiner in one instance and to encourage an early retirement in another.

Information issues at East Birmingham College are very different but a similar picture of a mixture of top-down and bottom-up strategies emerges. One of the problems was that the college had extended the flexibility of its curriculum – notably by introducing a number of smaller, OCN-accredited units – but found that student achievement was being under-recorded. The solution was a mixture of prescription, exhortation, encouragement and support driven by a Student Achievement Unit. This is discussed in the case study overleaf.

Case Study 17. Student Achievement Unit at East Birmingham College

Problems

- Administrative failures meant that some students were not entered, not assessed, or not credited for their achievement.
- Some students were not enrolled at all on their courses.
- Multiple qualifications were sometimes not recorded.
- Funding for 'other' qualifications was not claimed.
- There were particular concerns at entry/foundation level where up to 50% of achievements were not being recorded for some units.

Applied strategy

- Set up a Student Achievement Unit that:
  - Collects data on all student achievements
  - Confirms retention/destination data
  - Confirms the validity of the achievement data
  - Produces various reports e.g. publication of information about student achievements (PISA), Department for Education and Employment (DfEE) and FEFC reports
  - Confirms the college's final claim for funding units
  - Produces an achievement profile for each group of students on each course that includes:
    - A list of all students
    - Achievement and destination information for each student
    - National benchmark data
    - Data from the previous two years
    - A list of continuing students
    - The name of the member of staff responsible for the group.

Outcomes

- Instances of the 'let's say syndrome' (i.e. reporting based largely on conjecture) have been replaced by a focus on gathering accurate data.
- Both achievement and the recording of achievement have been improved.
- Targets are being set to 'meet or beat' national average targets and/or improve on previous performance.
- Achievement rates have increased as shown in the following table:

Figure 22. Achievement rates at East Birmingham College (1995 and 1998)

Achievement rates	1995	1998
GCSE	50·0	59·3
A-level	72·9	75·5
BTEC National	78·6	77·9
GNVQ Foundation	35·7	70·2
GNVQ Intermediate	43·7	62·6
GNVQ Advanced	62·5	75·2
HNC	78·4	93·1
All NVQs	59·1	64·9

The work of the Student Achievement Unit is being complemented by the introduction of senior management team 'buddies' (who support middle managers) and the preparation of checklists and prompts for course tutors, an example of which is given in Appendix 5·2.

Other initiatives that both control the collection of data and empower staff in their use of it include:

- The appointment of a student tracking officer (Barking College)
- The implementation of ICT-based tracking systems (Basford Hall College, East Birmingham College)
- ICT-based registration (Huddersfield New College)
- On-line access to national benchmark data (FEFC) and value added data (ALIS) (Huddersfield New College)

In view of the earlier discussion on adult student achievement, it is worth noting that similar strategies to collect accurate data, clarify roles and responsibilities and develop the capacity of tutors, managers and governors to understand, interpret, research and work with their own information, have been implemented at Richmond Adult and Community College.

Research

There has been considerable discussion over the last two years regretting the lack of a 'research culture' in further education and encouraging its development (FEDA, 1998a, 1999). There is substantial evidence that colleges are increasingly basing their improvement strategies on research of two main varieties:

- Problem diagnosis: college-based research to ascertain what is not working and why, often supplemented by the use of research from elsewhere
- The development of solutions using action research as a vehicle to define, monitor and evaluate solutions.

The action research approach has been examined in the previous chapter in the context of measures to motivate and develop staff. It is worth emphasising some of the salient features of action research applied to problem diagnosis:

- All of the colleges under review went through some sort of analytical and reflective exercise, even if only as part of their normal course review and/or self-assessment processes.
- More than one-third of colleges undertook a specific research exercise with designated responsibilities, timescales and reporting mechanisms.
- College research efforts were located on a spectrum which extends from relatively informal consideration of immediately available quantitative and qualitative data to more formal research exercises often led by project teams.
- More formal research efforts usually combine the analysis of available performance information and student evaluations with additional research gathered through staff and student surveys, focus groups and a more sophisticated analysis of data already held on MIS.
- Most of this college research is internally generated and consumed and does not enter the public domain.
- Occasionally, colleges make use of external researchers and consultants, notably from FEDA, but more often they do not.
- Like the improvement strategies themselves, the research activities that support them are led by a variety of college staff from principals to teachers and from heads of student services to curriculum managers.

Key points

- The way that strategies to raise achievement are inspired, researched, designed, implemented and evaluated varies considerably from college to college and even within the same college.
- In some colleges, change is being inspired and led by senior managers; in others by departmental heads or course teams.

- Leadership from the top appears to be particularly important in ensuring that improvement efforts take place across an institution, empowering and supporting such efforts and providing an information infrastructure.
- Most strategies to raise achievement also exhibit an inclusive or shared approach, typically embodied in cross-college task, implementation or support groups.
- Successful strategies that have been implemented over several years are developed and implemented within an action research framework and evolve over time.
- Elements of control and devolution or empowerment co-exist; the first tends to be associated with management information systems and procedures; the second with the interpretation and use of data produced by MIS.
- Many colleges have also developed significant centrally driven (and cross-college) strategies such as the introduction of target minimum grades or the redesign of threshold or tutorial processes. Where they exist, these initiatives are often planned and implemented with the assistance of a task or project group.
- The process of improving achievement almost invariably includes a research phase which sometimes takes the form of an extensive data-gathering and analytical exercise but more often involves a closer and more rigorous analysis and interrogation of existing quantitative and qualitative data already held by the college, department or team.

Summary: Key points

Beliefs about student achievement: key points

- Student achievement is a hotly contested and controversial subject that inspires strongly held beliefs and some myths.
- The views that raising achievement is not compatible with widening participation or improving retention are not supported by the evidence.
- Available evidence also contradicts the belief that demographic factors (such as social class) largely determine achievement in colleges.
- Substantial improvements in achievement have been made notwithstanding the different degrees of difficulty associated with different subjects, syllabi or awarding body, for the same type of qualification.
- It is the application of reasonably well-known principles of teaching, curriculum design and management, rather than the charismatic personalities of individual teachers or principals, that have the most effect on achievement.
- There is no universal remedy or hard-and-fast set of rules. The development and implementation of strategies are highly specific to the context of the college, department and often the course itself.

Student motivation: key points

- Colleges are seeking to increase achievement via strategies that promote extrinsic and intrinsic student motivation.
- Strategies to increase extrinsic motivation include prizes and ceremonies, parental involvement and student learning contracts and (the often associated) disciplinary procedures.
- Efforts by colleges to increase intrinsic motivation are mostly connected to curriculum design, teaching, formative assessment and tutoring.
- Some colleges are experimenting with specific interventions to enhance intrinsic motivation through peer support, to empower students in their career choices and to develop the career relevance of programmes.
- Monitoring and following up attendance often forms part of strategies to increase extrinsic motivation. Some colleges are experimenting with student self-monitoring of attendance.

Value added: key points

- Value added approaches are proving popular with students, parents, teachers and curriculum managers.
- The aspects of value added approaches that are particularly effective include setting and reviewing target minimum grades, monitoring and action planning student progress and using the information to inform the management of teaching and the curriculum.
- The use of value added approaches is becoming increasingly widespread in the A-level curriculum and, in some colleges, is associated with substantial improvements in A-level achievement.
- Colleges are making use of both nationally available (ALIS) and home-grown (ALPS) approaches.
- Colleges have experienced difficulties in trying to extend similar methods to vocational qualifications, notably GNVQs.
- Some colleges have pioneered formative value added processes and student profiling.
- Formative value added approaches in relation to vocational qualifications seem to have beneficial effects notwithstanding the absence of a firm statistical underpinning.
- There appears to be some further scope to bring together the statistical value added methods developed primarily in relation to A-levels and the student profiling and formative approaches developed mainly in vocational areas.

Tutoring: key points

- Tutoring is central to most college strategies to raise achievement.
- The largely pastoral focus for tutorials in some colleges is giving way to an emphasis on monitoring, reviewing and supporting overall student progress.
- Key elements in most tutoring systems include one-to-one tutorials, the skills and competencies of effective tutors and supportive administrative and managerial systems.
- Strategies to develop and improve tutoring are often centrally driven and contain a strong student services element.
- One of the main priorities for many colleges has been to improve the quality of tutoring by such means as staff development, role clarification, tutorial observations, improved administrative support and better cross-college coordination.

Teaching and pedagogy: key points

- Research on school effectiveness suggests that factors within education systems that impact most strongly on achievement are those that are closest to teaching and learning.
- There is a growing body of evidence derived principally from the school sector on the effectiveness of specific approaches to teaching and learning.
- For several years, colleges have been developing their teaching and learning strategies to improve achievement and retention, and a number of case studies are reported in this and other chapters of this guide.
- Teaching does not take place in isolation. The case studies suggest strong links between the review and development of teaching strategies, curriculum design and processes to inform, advise, guide and support students.
- There are a number of similarities between successful teaching strategies in colleges and those reported in the literature on schools; these include structured teaching, student-centred formative assessment, shared student-teacher ownership of learning, and differentiation.
- Colleges are at the leading edge of development in some aspects of pedagogy, notably: threshold and grouping procedures, tutoring and the devolution of curriculum strategy and design to teachers and teaching teams.
- Some successful strategies reported in schools could usefully be explored in colleges, particularly mastery learning, cooperative learning and the use of advance organisers.
- There are some characteristics that are often associated with effective college teaching but are not identified in the case studies and find little echo in the schools research. These include: teacher enthusiasm, varied teaching strategies, good subject knowledge, high quality teaching materials, and frequent checks on student learning. This is not to say that these aspects of teaching or pedagogy are unimportant but it may well suggest that they are necessary but not sufficient.
- Action research conducted along the lines suggested in this and later chapters will go some way to addressing the lack of empirical work to date on effective teaching in tertiary education generally, and in colleges in particular.

Curriculum strategy: key points

- Curriculum strategies to raise achievement are similar to those developed to improve retention. Specifically, colleges are continuing to review their curriculum offer to introduce new courses and new types of course and to withdraw from inappropriate or ineffective types of provision (even in the face of continuing market demand).
- Other common strategies include: unitisation and modularisation, the division of terms into blocks for learning and catch-up weeks, greater flexibility through open learning and resource-based learning and adjustments to timetabling.
- Timetabling issues remain controversial, with full-time programmes being arranged over five, four, three and even two days per week.
- A tentative inference is that the management of the teaching week needs to consider five main issues: the needs of students; student learning skills, curriculum design; teaching strategies; the nature and level of the programme.
- Increasingly, colleges are addressing basic and key skills needs as part of a continuum of study skills development rather than as discrete issues. Within such a continuum, substantial effort is being put into diagnosing needs early on, expanding provision to meet identified needs and ensuring that students make optimal use of available support.
- A range of techniques is being used to make basic and key skills support more effective, including integration, contextualisation, additional staffing, enhanced tutoring, monitoring and target-setting, and the training of teachers.

Adult achievement: key points

- Discussions about adult achievement are often polarised between those who see it as unproblematic and those who detect ambivalence, anxiety, lack of confidence or antagonism towards assessment and accreditation among adult students.
- Unless this issue can be resolved, it threatens to undermine the Government's policy to widen participation and promote lifelong learning.
- Analysis of the problem suggests that a focus of attention for colleges should be adult learners who may be relatively well motivated to learn but have little motivation to gain a qualification.
- Assessment techniques and accreditation frameworks have already been created which can provide 'student-friendly' assessment opportunities.
- There is a growing body of quantitative research (mainly from the school sector) and action research (mainly from the adult and higher education sectors) that this type of student-centred assessment motivates students and promotes effective learning.
- There are tensions between policy objectives to widen participation and provide lifelong learning on the one hand and improve audit and financial control on the other.
- These tensions appear to be impacting on the development of programmes aimed at adults who are least highly motivated to achieve qualifications.

Support for achievement: key points

- Support for achievement encompasses all those processes that help to place and support students on programmes of study: information, advice, guidance, recruitment and selection, careers education, initial screening and testing, induction, arrangements for course transfer and student support.
- The case studies in preceding chapters on teaching and curriculum strategy usually include changes to the management of this learning support.
- The colleges included in the research have changed, developed and improved their threshold procedures intended to ensure that students are appropriately placed on courses.
- The range of strategies extends from initial information and advice through interviews and relationship building prior to enrolment, to induction, extended diagnostic testing and course transfer arrangements.
- Some colleges have blurred the distinction between guidance, taster, induction and diagnostic processes through the introduction of freestanding modules leading to alternative programmes.
- Student Services functions often play a key role in the design, development and implementation of strategies aimed at improving student achievement.

Staff motivation: key points

- Staff motivation is a key element in strategies to improve achievement.
- The main strategies to motivate staff seem to be: team development; information and awareness raising; continuing professional development; efforts to reduce bureaucracy; a shared approach to the management of change.
- Considerable attention is being given to develop effective teaching teams and, to a lesser extent, devolve managerial responsibility to such teams.
- Information and awareness raising strategies have been used to share good practice from within and outside a college and to challenge untested assumptions about student achievement.
- Continuing professional development is important – partly for its own sake and partly to motivate staff.
- In this context the most prevalent forms of continuing professional development include action research, the observation of teaching and learning and mentoring.
- Many colleges are also attempting to motivate staff by reducing bureaucracy and red tape.

Processes for raising achievement: key points

- The way that strategies to raise achievement are inspired, researched, designed, implemented and evaluated varies considerably from college to college and even within the same college.
- In some colleges, change is being inspired and led by senior managers; in others by departmental heads or course teams.
- Leadership from the top appears to be particularly important in ensuring that improvement efforts take place across an institution, empowering and supporting such efforts and providing an information infrastructure.
- Most strategies to raise achievement also exhibit an inclusive or shared approach, typically embodied in cross-college task, implementation or support groups.
- Successful strategies that have been implemented over several years are developed and implemented within an action research framework and evolve over time.
- Elements of control and devolution or empowerment co-exist; the first tends to be associated with management information systems and procedures; the second with the interpretation and use of data produced by MIS.
- Many colleges have also developed significant centrally-driven (and cross-college) strategies such as the introduction of target minimum grades or the redesign of threshold or tutorial processes. Where they exist, these initiatives are often planned and implemented with the assistance of a task or project group.
- The process of improving achievement almost invariably includes a research phase which sometimes takes the form of an extensive data-gathering and analytical exercise but more often involves a closer and more rigorous analysis and interrogation of existing quantitative and qualitative data already held by the college, department or team.

References

AoC. *Standards fund: response to FEFC Circular 99/12.* AoC, 1999.

Astor H. *The introduction of learning outcomes.* Mosaic, 1995.

Barnard P, Dixon S. *Value added: beyond A-levels to vocational programmes?* FEDA, 1998.

Basic Skills Agency. *Staying the course: the relationship between basic skills support, drop-out, retention and management – further education colleges.* BSA, 1997.

Bathmaker A-M, Parsons J, Avis J. *Whither time? Towards an analysis of the labour process with FE.* University of Wolverhampton, paper presented at BERA Conference 2–5 September 1999.

Beinart S, Smith P. *National adult learning survey 1997.* DfEE, 1998.

Biggs J, Moore P. *The process of learning (3rd edition).* London: Prentice Hall, 1993.

Black P, Wiliam D. *Assessment and classroom learning. Assessment inEducation.* 1998; 5 (1).

Brennan J, Little B. *A review of work-based learning in higher education.* DfEE, 1996.

Brighouse T, Woods D. *How to improve your school.* London: Routledge, 1999.

Brown S, Baume D. *Learning contracts (2 volumes).* London: SCED, 1992.

Cohen L, Manion L. *Research methods in education (4th edition).* London: Routledge, 1994.

Conway, K. *A-level performance systems (ALPS).* Greenhead College, 1997.

Creemers B. *The effective classroom.* London: Cassell, 1994.

Crowder M, Pupynin K. *The motivation to train.* Department of Employment, 1993.

Davies P. *Learning and earning: report of a research project on the impact of paid employment on young people in full-time education.* FEDA, 1999.

Davis V *et al.* Assessment issues in further education. FEDA, 1995.

DfEE. *GCSE to GCE A/AS value added; briefing for schools and colleges.* DfEE, 1995.

DfEE. *Review of qualifications for 16–19-year-olds (The Dearing Report).* DfEE, 1996.

DfEE. *Improving literacy and numeracy, a fresh start (The Moser Report).* DfEE, 1999.

Dolan J, Cantley A (eds). *Students supporting students.* Birmingham: SEDA, 1998.

Donley J, Napper R. *Assessment matters in adult learning.* NIACE and Oxfordshire Community Education, 1999.

FEDA. *Implementing college strategic plans.* FEDA, 1995.

FEDA. *Non-completion of GNVQs.* FEDA, 1998.

FEDA. *College research.* FEDA, Spring 1998a.

FEDA. *College research 3(1).* FEDA, 1999.

FEDA. *National standards for adult literacy and numeracy: general questionnaire.* Draft. FEDA, 1999a.

FEFC. *GCSE in the further education sector. National survey report.* FEFC, 1997.

FEFC. *Basic Education: curriculum area survey report.* FEFC, 1998.

FEFC. *Widening participation: national survey report.* FEFC (forthcoming), 2000.

FEFC. *Applications for funding for non-schedule 2 pilot projects.* Circular 99/16. FEFC, 1999a.

FEFC. *Effective self-assessment (1998–99).* FEFC, 1999b.

FEFC. *Council News. 28 May.* FEFC, 1999c.

FEFC. *Schedule 2. Circular 99/10.* FEFC, 1999d.

FEU. *Securing adequate provision for adult returners.* FEU, 1994.

Fallow S, Ahmet K (eds). *Inspiring students; case studies in motivating the learner.* Kogan Page, 1999.

Fitz-Gibbon C, Vincent L. *Difficulties regarding subject difficulties: developing reasonable explanation for observable data.* Oxford Review of Education. 1997; 23 (3).

Fitz-Gibbon C. *The value added national project, final report.* London: SCAA, 1997.

Foster P, Howard U, Reisenberger A. *A sense of achievement: outcomes of adult learning.* FEDA, 1997.

Hayes A. *'Standards' and the measurement of the learning outcomes of adult students in further education.* Kensington and Chelsea College, paper presented at FERN Conference, 9–10 December 1999.

House of Commons. *Access for all.* Education and Employment Committee, minutes of evidence, 16 February. London: Stationery Office, 1999.

Joslin, H. *How student services can help to improve retention.* Presented at FEDA Conference, 13 April 1999.

Joyce B, Calhoun E, Hopkins D. *The new structure of school improvement.* Open University, 1999.

Kember D. *The use of a model to derive interventions which might reduce drop-out from distance education.* Higher Education. 1990; vol 20.

Kennedy H. *Learning works; widening participation in further education.* FEFC, 1997.

Lamping A, Ball C. *Maintaining motivation: Strategies for improving retention rates in adult language classes.* Centre for Information on Language Teaching and Research, 1996.

Lavender P. *Learning outcomes: towards a synthesis of progress.* NIACE, paper presented at FERN Conference 9–10 December 1999.

Leney T, Lucas N, Taubman D. *Learning funding: the impact of FEFC funding on twelve FE colleges.* NATFHE and Institute of Education, 1998.

Liverpool Community College Courier. Staff magazine. Liverpool Community College, 1998.

Martinez P. *Student retention: case studies of strategies that work.* FEDA, 1996.

Martinez P. *Improving student retention; a guide to successful strategies.* FEDA, 1997.

Martinez P. *Aiming at achievement.* FEDA, 1999a.

Martinez P. *Learning from continuing professional development.* FEDA, 1999b.

Martinez P, Houghton J, Krupska M. *Staff development for student retention in further and adult education.* FEDA, 1998.

Martinez P, Munday F. *9000 voices.* FEDA, 1998.

Martinez P, Pepler G. *Reducing bureaucratic burdens on lecturers.* FEDA, 1999.

Mortimore, P (ed). *Understanding pedagogy and its impact on learning.* London: Sage, 1999.

Payne J. *Qualifications between 16 and 18: a comparison of achievements on routes beyond compulsory schooling (England and Wales: Youth Cohort Study, vol 32).* London: Employment Department, 1995.

Petty G. *Teaching Today (2nd edition).* London: Stanley Thornes, 1998.

Pierce J. *Use of unitised learner pathways (unpublished FEDA report RP163).* FEDA, 1998.

Pitcher T. *Whole college strategies to raise achievement (2)*. FEDA Conference presentation, 25 June 1998.

Robertson C. *Work-based learning contracts*. London: HMSO, 1992.

Robson J. *A profession in crisis: status, culture and identity in the further education college. Journal of Vocational Education and Training*, 1998; 50 (4).

Sammons P, Hillman J, Mortimore P. *Key characteristics of effective schools; a review of schools effectiveness research*. London: Institute of Education/Ofsted, 1997.

Scheerens J, Bosker R. *The foundations of educational effectiveness*. London: Pergamon, 1997.

Somekh B *et al. Improving college effectiveness*. FEDA, 1999.

South East Essex College. *Retention analysis for the period September 1997 to June 1998. (unpublished internal report)*. South East Essex College, 1998.

Spours K (ed). *Value added strategies for raising attainment and achievement; developments in Essex*. London: Institute of Education, 1996.

Spours K, Hodgson A. *Value added and raising attainment: a formative approach*. London: Institute of Education, 1996.

Staff College/FEU. *Strategic planning handbook*. Staff College/FEU, 1994.

Stent S. *The relationship between the work of the Key Skills Centre, retention and achievement*. Barking College, 1998.

Stephenson J, Laycock M (eds). *Using learning contracts in higher education*. London: Kogan Page, 1993.

Visscher A (ed). Managing schools towards high performance. Lisse, The Netherlands, Swets and Zeitlinger, 1999.

Wang M, Haertel G, Walberg H. *Toward a knowledge base for school learning*. Review of Educational Research. 1993; 63 (3).

Warren T. *People management and corporate success*. College Research (Summer) FEDA, 1998.

Watson K. *Improving retention and achievement in A-levels*. FEDA Conference presentation, 11 February 1998.

WEA. *Learning outcomes strategy; District monitoring procedure*. WEA, 1998.

WEA. *Describing learning outcomes in WEA courses; notes for tutors 1999–2000*. WEA, 1999.

Yarrow K, Esland G. *The changing role of the professional in the new further education (unpublished paper, part of PHD)*, 1998.

Acronyms

ACET (Gloucestershire) Adult and Continuing Education and Training
ALIS A-level information system
ALPS A-level performance system
BSA Basic Skills Agency
BTEC Business and Technology Education Council
CITB Construction Industry Training Board
CPD continuing professional development
DfEE Department for Education and Employment
FTE full-time equivalent
GNVQ general national and vocational qualification
HMI Her Majesty's Inspector
HND higher national diploma
HoD head of department
ICT information communications technology
ILT information and learning technology
IT information technology
LEA local education authority
LMW learner management week
MIS management information system
NIACE National Institute of Adult Continuing Education
NOCN National Open College Network
OCN Open College Network
OMR optical mark reader
PISA publication of information about student achievements
SLDD students with learning difficulties and/or disabilities
SPOP student perception of programme
STAR Student Tracking and Achievement Record
WEA Workers' Educational Association

Appendices

Raising achievement: outcomes of strategies

Faced with a huge and growing volume of information, advice and sometimes exhortation, teachers, support staff and managers are entitled to ask 'Does it work?' This appendix summarises the scope and outcomes of the strategies reviewed in this guide and serves as a brief introduction to the work of the different colleges.

Arnold and Carlton College

Scope: Music Technology.
Outcomes: Retention and achievement rates were almost doubled in a year.

Barking College

Scope: Key Skills Centre.
Outcomes: Students attending the Key Skills Centre are significantly more likely to stay on course (86%) and achieve (81%) than those not attending.

Barnsley College

Scope: Creative Arts.
Outcomes: Achievement rates in 1998 were 63% and 82% for intermediate and advanced students, respectively, compared with national averages of 48% and 67%. Retention rates have improved from 66% to 86% (intermediate) and from 61% to 82% (advanced, Year 1).

Basford Hall College (now part of New College Nottingham)

Scope: Careers education and guidance programme targeted initially on full-time programmes with poor retention rates; subsequently adopted more widely.
Outcomes: Up to 100% retention on some courses that previously experienced poor retention rates; very positive staff and student evaluations.

Bridgwater College

Scope: Learning support for all students.
Outcomes: Following additional support and close monitoring, students most at risk ('amber alert' students) have better retention rates than those not at risk. From a sample of 101 students on intermediate level programmes, 83% of amber alert students completed compared with 69% of other intermediate students.

Burnley College

Scope: Whole college.
Outcomes: Start-to-finish retention rates on one- and two-year courses increased from 65% and 63% to 78% and 80% (1998) over three years.

Bury College

Scope: GNVQ Intermediate Business.
Outcomes: Retention improved from 75% (1995) to 80% (1999). Achievement improved from 53% to 66% in the same period.

Canterbury College

Scope: Student services, as part of a college-wide strategy.

Outcomes: Across the college retention rates have increased to over 90%, with particular improvements in hairdressing and in motor vehicle courses.

Carmel College

Scope: All students (mainly full-time A-level students).

Outcomes: Average A-level point scores per student have increased from 12·0 (1992) to 21·9 (1998) against a modest increase in average GCSE point scores. Retention rates for full-time students are over 93%.

City College Norwich

Scope: Modular open access programme for adult learners.

Outcomes: 8% improvement in achievement rates; increased focus on inclusive learning approaches and introduction of additional pre-foundation modules.

Dewsbury College

Scope: Development of Maths, English and IT study centres.

Outcomes: Significant take-up of study centre opportunities beyond timetabled attendance. A–C grades: 55% for GCSE Maths; 67% for GCSE English and 95% pass rates for OCN units. Beacon Award for Maths in 1996 and a Grade 1 inspection for Maths in 1994.

East Birmingham College (now part of City College Birmingham)

Scope: Raising student achievement levels across the whole college.

Outcomes: FEFC Performance Indicator 4 for all student achievements has increased from 63% for 1996–97 to 75% for 1997–98. The A-level pass rate increased from 72·9% in 1995 to 80·2% in 1999. The GCSE pass rate increased from 50% to 67·5% in the same period.

Epping Forest College

Scope: Computing courses for part-time adult students.

Outcomes: The withdrawal rate by mid-November reduced from 13·7% (1998) to 5% (1999).

Gloucestershire Adult and Continuing Education and Training (ACET)

Scope: Adult Education Service (non-Schedule 2 only) with delivery contracted out to four FE colleges, WEA, Gloucestershire Federation of Women's Institutes and University of Bristol.

Outcomes: (1997–98 and 1998–99):

- 79% attendance rate
- All retained students achieved their learning outcomes; 8283 credits were achieved by ACET funded students
- 91% retention rate
- 96% of students felt that they had gained greatly from their course.

Great Yarmouth College

Scope: Whole college.

Outcomes: Full-time retention rates improved from 84% to 87% (1996–97); part-time retention rates stayed the same at 88%. Achievement on long qualifications improved from 76% to 83% in the same period (and from 79% to 82% across all qualifications).

Greenhead College

Scope: All students (mainly full-time A-level students).

Outcomes: Average A-level point scores bear comparison with those of elite private schools. Average A-level point scores increased from 12 points per student in 1987 to an average of 26 points in 1999.

Hartlepool College

Scope: Whole-college unified tutorial system together with other measures to improve retention and achievement.

Outcomes: Between 1995 and 1997, achievement rates increased by between 11% (GNVQs and precursors) and 21% (A and A/S level). Attendance rates increased by 8% over the same period.

Huddersfield New College

Scope: GNVQs.

Outcomes:

Figure 23. GNVQ outcomes 1998

Level	Enrolments	Completion %	All achievements %	Merits and distinctions %
Foundation	34	82	93	76
Intermediate	93	89	94	64
Advanced	174	88	78	68

Lewes Tertiary College

Scope: A-level and GNVQ Advanced.

Outcomes: Year-on-year increase in A–E passes in A-levels to 89% (1993 to 1998). Increase in average A-level point scores from 10·9 to 14·9. Incremental increases in GNVQ pass rates to 82% (1998).

Liverpool Community College

Scope: Targeted interventions on designated courses from every programme area and a cross-college initiative to improve tutoring.

Outcomes: Retention on all courses increased from 76% to 85% over a three-year period.

Llandrillo College

Scope: Cross-college mentoring for course teams.

Outcomes: The pass rate in full-time A-levels increased from 83% (1998) to 89·5% (1999).

Lowestoft College
Scope: Leisure & Tourism Advanced GNVQ.
Outcomes: Retention increased from a low of 54% (1996) to 92% (1999). All students completed two-thirds of the full award in Year 1. All except one student passed four end tests by the end of Year 1. Efficiency gains: 2·3 full-time equivalent staff generated 3·5k funding units.

Luton Sixth Form College
Scope: A-level and GNVQ Intermediate.
Outcomes: Improved UCAS point score equivalent to 0·5 of an A-level grade (mainly among middle ability groupings achieving Bs and Cs rather than Cs and Ds). Average student achievement above ALIS predictions; significantly better retention on GNVQ intermediate programmes compared with previous GCSE resit programmes.

North Warwickshire & Hinckley College
Scope: Hairdressing and Beauty Therapy.
Outcomes: Average retention rates increased from 80·5% to 88·5% (1997 to 1999); achievement rates increased from 78% to 89% (1997–99).

Oxford College of FE
Scope: Faculty of Languages and Humanities.
Outcomes: Improved pass rates in most Media Studies courses and Humanities A-levels. A large number of OCN units being achieved by part-time adult language students.

Palmer's College
Scope: Initial focus on students at risk of withdrawing from or failing their A-level.
Outcomes: Students gaining A-levels an average of two points higher than predicted on the basis of GCSE scores and 1·9 points higher than predicted by teachers.

Reading College and School of Art and Design
Scope: Tutoring for full-time students.
Outcomes: Up to 40% improvement in retention rates 1997–99. Substantial improvement in achievement rates in engineering and motor vehicle courses.

Regent College
Scope: Whole college.
Outcomes: Improved retention rates from 86% to 91% (1997–98). Heightened staff awareness of issues; parents particularly appreciative of closer contact with college on attendance issues.

Richmond Adult and Community College
Scope: Whole college.
Outcomes: Average pass rates have increased to 84·7%.

Runshaw College

Scope: Whole college.

Outcomes: Success rates (achievements in relation to enrolments) increased by 10% (1996–97) and 5% (1997–98). Retention rates increased by 5% (1997–98); average attendance rates are 90%.

Solihull College

Scope: Teacher Training Department.

Outcomes: Average retention rates are 91% (1998) and pass rates are 90%. The success ratio (achievements over enrolments) averages at 77%.

Solihull Sixth Form College

Scope: A-level History students.

Outcomes: The main improvement has occurred among students who previously were achieving D and E grades and who are now achieving B and C grades. History Department results were once below and are now above the average for the sixth form college sector. More than 80% of students achieve or exceed their A-level predicted grade for history.

South Birmingham College

Scope: Childhood Studies.

Outcomes: Retention averaged 85% across the department; three out of five Year 1 groups had retention rates of 90% or more.

South East Essex College

Scope: Whole college.

Outcomes: The largest group of successful GNVQ candidates in England in 1997: 550 advanced level and 370 intermediate level candidates. Average A-level point scores have increased from nine to 15 points between 1994 and 1997. A-level pass rates have increased from 55% (1990) to 84% (1997) and from below to above national average for FE colleges.

South Nottingham College

Scope: Cross-college strategies and local strategies in particular curriculum areas.

Outcomes: Between 1997 and 1998, the college moved from below national average (for GFE colleges) to above average for long courses. There were particularly significant improvements in A-level Sociology.

Sparsholt College of Agriculture and Horticulture

Scope: Whole college.

Outcomes: Achievement rates on full-time courses have been static for one-year courses but rising for two- and three-year courses (1995–97).

Suffolk College

Scope: Restructuring into small curriculum/management centres with clearer focus on quality.

Outcomes: More than two-thirds of college provision in top 25% of FE sector colleges for retention and achievement; year-on-year improvements in achievement in National Diplomas, A-levels and First Diplomas/Intermediate GNVQs.

Sutton Coldfield College
Scope: GNVQ programmes.
Outcomes: Achievement rates for Advanced GNVQs are above national average for the FE sector.

Telford College of Arts and Technology
Scope: Whole-college curriculum model.
Outcomes: Improved retention and achievement; higher standards of student work; well received by students and staff.

Tower Hamlets College
Scope: A-levels.
Outcomes: Average point scores for 16–19-year-olds taking two or more A-levels have increased from 8·2 (1995) to 10·9 (1998). The percentage of applicants progressing to higher education has risen from 63% (1996) to 83% (1998). Retention rates for the two years of the A-level programme are 67% (1996–98).

Uxbridge College
Scope: GNVQ Foundation Level.
Outcomes:

Figure 24. Retention and achievement rates for GNVQ Foundation at Uxbridge College

	1995/6	1996/7	1997/8
Retention (%)	50	85	87
Achievement (%)	47	84	100

Walsall College of Arts and Technology
Scope: Adult students.
Outcomes: At the end of the pilot period, 95% of the first cohort of 808 students had completed or were continuing with their programme. Out of the completers, more than 80% had achieved.

West Herts College
Scope: Leisure & Tourism GNVQs (Travel Option).
Outcomes: Retention rates improved to 78% (intermediate) and to 86% and 97% (Year 1 and Year 2, advanced, respectively). Pass rates increased to 74% (intermediate) and 97% (advanced). All Year 1 advanced students progressed to the Year 2 in 1998.

West Kent College
Scope: A variety of different initiatives mainly across the college.
Outcomes: Improvements in retention and achievement are associated in a number of courses with closer on-programme monitoring. An increase in retention in the Access programme from 85% (1995–96) to 97% (1998–99) is largely associated with a curtailment of late entry.

Wirral Metropolitan College

Scope: Leisure and Tourism GNVQs.

Outcomes: Positive feedback from students. Increased numbers of students progressing to employment in the leisure and tourism sector or to HNDs.

Wulfrun College (now part of Wolverhampton College)

Scope: A-levels; GCSE English and Maths GNVQs.

Outcomes: 9% improvement in GNVQ Advanced pass rates from 1996–1997. GCSE English and Maths achievement rates are above the average for FE colleges. Significant improvement in A-level pass rates in Science subjects (Chemistry, Physics and Biology) 1998–1999.

Yale College

Scope: Biology Department.

Outcomes: A–E passes in Human Biology have increased from 48% (1993) to 77% (1998). A–E passes in A-level Biology have increased from 84% to 97% in the same period and A–C passes in Biology from 51% to 71%.

Supplementary materials relating to teaching and pedagogy

Appendix 2·1

History Department, Solihull Sixth Form College:
Planning sheet for an essay addressing a 'why?' question

QUESTION

- KEY 'INSTRUCTION' WORDS
- THEREFORE TYPE OF QUESTION?
- ANY TERMS/NAMES/DATES NEED EXPLAINING?

INTRODUCTION

FIRST SENTENCE OF FIRST PARAGRAPH

(HAVE YOU MADE YOUR KEY POINT?)
DEVELOPMENT/EXPLANATION OF POINT?

EVIDENCE TO SUPPORT YOUR ARGUMENT?
1.
2.
3.

CHECK: HAVE YOU REFERRED BACK TO QUESTION/LINKED POINT EXPLICITY TO QUESTION?
LINK TO NEXT PARAGRAPH /POINT?

FIRST SENTENCE OF SECOND PARAGRAPH

HAVE YOU MADE YOUR KEY POINT?
DEVELOPMENT/EXPLANATION OF POINT?

EVIDENCE TO SUPPORT YOUR ARGUMENT?
1.
2.
3.

CHECK: HAVE YOU REFERRED BACK TO QUESTION/LINKED POINT EXPLICITY TO QUESTION?

LINK TO NEXT PARAGRAPH POINT?

History Department, Solihull Sixth Form College:
Planning for an essay addressing an 'arguments' question

QUESTION:		KEY INSTRUCTION WORDS: How far How successfully To what extent Assess Discuss Do you agree	
YES/AGREE ARGUMENTS	PRIORITY ORDER	NO/DISAGREE ARGUMENTS	PRIORITY ORDER

NOW CHOOSE A TWO-PART OR SIMULTANEOUS APPROACH

ARE THERE ENOUGH LINKS BETWEEN THE 'YES' AND 'NO' ARGUMENTS TO ALLOW A SIMULTANEOUS APPROACH'

NOW FIND EXAMPLES/EVIDENCE TO BACK UP EACH OF YOUR ARGUMENTS:

Appendix 2·3

**History Department, Solihull Sixth Form College,
Student Self-assessment Sheet**

HISTORY DEPARTMENT, SOLIHULL SIXTH FORM COLLEGE
STUDENT SELF-ASSESSMENT SHEET

NAME:	MY ALIS TARGET GRADE:	MARK & GRADE RECEIVED FOR THIS WORK:
ESSAY QUESTION *or* TITLE OF ASSIGNMENT :	DATE:	
READING/PREPARATION DONE FOR THIS ASSIGNMENT:		
STUDENT SELF-ASSESSMENT ON THIS PIECE OF WORK *to be completed before handing work in*		
STUDENT COMMENT AFTER RECEIVING MARKED WORK BACK:		

History Department, Solihull Sixth Form College: Examples of exercises designed to encourage active learning, develop critical and analytical skills and make history enjoyable

Examples of exercises in modern British and European history

1 Group Work – research and presentations on Liberal Social Reforms

Class divided into four groups investigating reforms re:

- Young
- Old
- Sick
- Workers.

Using handout containing primary sources and relevant chapter in ... identify report back to whole class under headings:

- Problem
- Action
- Opposition
- Results.

Followed by class discussion – assessing success/failure of reforms in tackling problem of poverty.

2 Class debate – Was revolution unavoidable in Russia by 1914?

Preparation – four groups investigating:

- Economic
- Political arguments for and against.

Debate – four speakers – one from each group, one presenting:

- Economic argument for
- Economic argument against
- Political argument for
- Political argument against.

Open discussion followed by vote.

3 Posters – American Independence

Ratification of Constitution. Groups prepare campaign posters either for or against ratification.

4 Role play

Focus: 1914 Buckingham Palace Conference
Exercise: You are representing your group at the conference and your mission is to try and achieve your goal re.: Ireland and Home Rule by negotiation/dealing/threatening etc. with other groups.
Groups:

- King George V + Advisers
- Asquith, Lloyd George and Liberals
- Bonar Law + Conservatives
- Carson + Ulster Unionists
- Redmond + Irish Nationalists
- Irish Volunteers, IRB etc., Sinn Fein.

Appendix 3

Additional case studies on teaching and pedagogy

Appendix 3·1

Case Study: A-level Biology at Yale College, Wrexham

Problem

- A-level passes (A–E) declining from 88% to 74% (1992–95) and A–C passes declining from 54% to 49% over the same period.

Applied strategies

- Adopted a modular syllabus from 1997
- Made more time available to biology course team leader through creating course team leader roles for Human Biology (A/AS levels) and GCSE Biology
- Introduced value added formative assessment
- Created a staff/student liaison group involving a student representative from each teaching group
- Provided learning materials including a standardised collection of course handouts, previous examination questions and model answers and self-study booklets for a number of basic topics
- Introduced a course booklet containing the scheme of work, guidance on reading, assessment and exams, and information on career opportunities and module content
- The team leader for biology became an assistant examiner for A-level modular Biology.

Outcomes

- A-level passes at A–E have increased to between 91% and 98% for 1996–98 from 74% in 1995.
- A-level passes at A–C have risen to 71% in 1998 from 49% in 1995.

Case Study. Department of Early Childhood Studies: South Birmingham College

Background

The department had already put in place a variety of strategies to improve retention and achievement:

- Recruitment: early interviewing, maintaining links with applicants and early enrolment (before the summer break)
- Induction over several weeks to include initial testing (via Basic Skills Agency [BSA] instruments), an induction assignment and visits to work placement providers
- Regular (twice termly) course evaluations
- Monitoring and follow up of student absences
- Learning resources: a curriculum resource centre was developed in a converted classroom to provide help with assignments and aspects of programmes which some students found particularly difficult (such as theory or observation techniques), and contextualised support to develop literacy and numeracy skills
- A modular curricula with multiple start points.

Problems

- Across the department, average retention rates declined to around 80% in 1997–98 from a previous rate of more than 90%.
- Nothing had changed in the way that the department recruited, delivered programmes or monitored student progress and attendance.
- The only external change that could be identified was pressure from employment services staff on male unemployed students to withdraw from courses.
- Teaching teams concluded that the rise in drop-out was mainly associated with unrealistic expectations and lack of preparation on the part of some students.

Applied strategies

- Introduced interviewing in small teams (including the work placement officer) to ensure that students gained greater insight into the requirements of their courses and of the work placement
- Introduced standard interview questions and formats
- Provided follow-up newsletters and coffee mornings/afternoons for successful applicants
- Developed a common induction programme for two weeks across all programmes and levels, still including BSA tests and a mini-assignment
- Combined feedback from the mini-assignment with individual interviews for all 400 students leading to adjustments of the level of programme for some students and changes of course for others
- Followed up student absences more rapidly and involved the careers service in the event of persistent absence.

Outcomes

- Retention averaged 85% across the department; three out of five first-year groups had 90%+ retention.
- To monitor the impact of the new induction programme, staff recorded at interview which course candidates were likely to follow. Only 0.5% of students moved to alternative courses as a result of the BSA test and completion of an induction assignment.
- Only 10% of students (via the College Induction Survey) said that the induction did not help them to settle quickly into college. However, staff recorded a higher percentage of dislike for the style of induction at course review.
- Staff concluded that they are largely able to identify the appropriate course at interview.
- The Careers Service followed up students who left, to check reasons for leaving. Students gave the same reasons, implying that the departmental data capture system is working well.

Appendix 3·3

Case Study. Department of Hairdressing and Beauty Therapy at North Warwickshire and Hinckley College

Problems

- Poor retention in some courses (between 56% and 70%).
- 16–19-year-olds are more likely to drop-out than mature students (four times more likely in the case of 16-year-olds, and twice as likely in the case of 17 and 18-year-olds).
- Late applications and a previous history of withdrawal from courses provided good predictors of drop-out and most 16-year-olds had one or both characteristics.
- Lack of understanding on the part of many students as to the requirements and the content of the course for which they were applying.

Applied strategies

- Used panel interviewing for students who only put 'hairdressing' or 'beauty therapy' on their application form
- Introduced advice and guidance sessions for the more specialist part-time vocational programmes (mainly for older students)
- Targeted tutorial support towards identified categories of students at risk and brought the first tutorial forward to the third or fourth week of the programme
- Made attempts to involve parents and guardians more closely
- Improved the explanation of assignments and assessments and the provision of extra support, mainly for older part-time students
- Addressed issues of behaviour/performance in tutorials where these had sometimes been ignored previously (to foster 'good relationships')
- Provided additional personal tutorials for the six most-at-risk first year hairdressing student.
- Changed the timetabling to meet the needs of mature students on some courses
- Improved the presentation skills of some teachers (prompted by teaching observations)
- Introduced voluntary sessions during the summer to provide catch-up opportunities for some students and to maintain the momentum for some January/March starters
- Focused staff development on recognising at risk students and developing initiatives to improve the situation
- Negotiated clear targets for retention and achievement with the progïmme coordinators.

Outcomes

Since serious efforts to raise retention and achievement rates began, there have been measurable improvements to overall figures; also the clusters where performance was of particular concern have been brought into line with other provision.

Figure 25. Retention and achievement rates, Department of Hairdressing and Beauty Therapy

	Retention %	Achievement %
1996/97	80·5	78
1997/98	84·5	87
1998/99	88·5	89

Appendix 3·4

Case Study. GNVQs at Sutton Coldfield College

Problems

- Need to improve retention and achievement
- Desire to become a regional centre for GNVQ excellence
- Need to improve standards across the GNVQ curriculum.

Applied strategies

- Introduced well-developed diagnostic screening (using BSA instruments)
- Carried out additional testing of specific key skills and individual assessment interviews for foundation and intermediate level students
- Mapped assignments to avoid overload and redundancy
- Provided lucid assignment briefs to give a clear idea of what is expected, assessment criteria and key skills pointers
- Provided well-presented, bespoke assignments
- Grouped foundation level students into one department for cross c ollege foundation studies.
- Set up a GNVQ centre containing workstations, printers, CD-ROMs, Internet-connected personal computers, individual and group areas, a variety of learning materials and staffed by a supervisor, assistant and IT assistant
- Contextualised basic and key skills materials, offering both discrete and integrated delivery with clear allocation of responsibility
- Introduced formative student profiling
- Simplified and faster administration and attendance monitoring via information communications technology (ICT) applications
- Provided regular meeting slots for teams, where student progress and performance are standard items on the agenda
- Coordinated the strategies across the college to ensure common standards, to implement common requirements and, above all, to share best practice.

Outcomes

Achievement rates for Advanced GNVQ (and for a large cohort of students) are well above average for the FE sector.

Case Study. A-levels at Tower Hamlets College

Problems

- Poor attainment at GCSE in local schools (25% achieve A–C passes)
- Around 30% of students who are on A-level programmes have writing skills below Level 1
- Around 60% of A-level students have English as a second language
- Many students have had long periods of absence from school (and college) often due to extended visits to families overseas.

Applied strategies

- Offered careful pre-entry guidance via visits to Year 11 groups and college-based interviews and taster days during the summer
- Used BSA tests to identify learning support needs and numeracy, and communications workshops to identify the type of support required
- Set up a pastoral system unique within the college where tutor team leaders act as heads of year
- Maintained a stable team of experienced teachers
- Adopted modular curricula in some subjects
- Established a highly structured learning agreement and a disciplinary process that involves parents
- Provided regular monitoring and discussion of student progress via personal tutorials and the use of 'success action plans'
- Set up schemes for particular groups of students including Oxford, Cambridge and London School of Economics Access schemes, work experience in the city of London and a tutoring scheme delivered by A-level students in local schools.

Outcomes

- Average point scores for 16–19-year-olds taking two or more A-levels have increased from 8.2 (1995) to 10.9 (1998).
- The percentage of applicants progressing to higher education has risen from 63% in 1996 to 83% in 1998. Retention rates over the whole two years of the A-level programme are 67% (1996–98).

Appendix 4

Supplementary materials relating to curriculum strategy

Appendix 4·1

Bridgwater College: Retention 'amber alert' checklist

COURSE:

RETENTION: 'AMBER ALERT' CHECKLIST

How to Spot a Possible Early Leaver
(in use from admission - First Two-Way Reviews)

NAME	Late Application	Late Enrolment	Missed Induction	Below Entry Qualifications	Started a Course Before/Failed to Complete	(Previous) Erratic Attendance Record	Lateness	Late Submission of Work	Financial/ Social/ Domestic Pressure	Lack of Motivation	Other Factors*

More than 2 xs = potential early leaver. Student needs extra front-loaded tutorial support.
*Courses to identify own criteria.

Bridgwater College: School report to be completed by school staff

PART 2
School Report to be completed by School Staff

PLEASE CIRCLE THE APPROPRIATE GRADE FOR THE FOLLOWING

(1 = excellent 5 = poor)

	Excellent				Poor
Attitude	1	2	3	4	5
Effort	1	2	3	4	5
Attendance	1	2	3	4	5
Punctuality	1	2	3	4	5

EXPECTED PERFORMANCE IN GCSE EXAMINATIONS

Subject	Estimated GCSE grade or grade already achieved	Subject	Estimated GCSE grade or grade already achieved

ACADEMIC POTENTIAL Please tick box as appropriate.

He/she should apply for a more demanding course

He/she should find the course well suited to his/her capabilities

He/she has overestimated his/her capabilities and should consider a less demanding course

Unable to comment

DOES THE APPLICANT HAVE ANY PARTICULAR ADDITIONAL NEEDS FOR WHICH THE COLLEGE SHOULD PROVIDE? If Yes, please give details.

GENERAL REMARKS

Name
(Please print)

Position

Signature

Date

Appendix 4·3

Bridgwater College: Learner services – additional support needs

Bridgwater College – Learner Services
ADDITIONAL SUPPORT NEEDS

STAFF SUPPORTING STUDENTS 1:1 GUIDELINES

Student's Name:	
Course:	Tutor:
Contracted Hours:	Subject:
Date Commenced:	Date Completed:
Time:	Venue:
Lecturer:	Lecturer's Signature:

DATE	SUBJECT COVERED	COMMENTS	Student's Initials

REVIEW 1

Lecturer's Comments	Student's Comments	Date:
		Action

Lecturer's Signature: Student's Signature:

REVIEW 2

Lecturer's Comments	Student's Comments	Date:
		Action

Lecturer's Signature: Student's Signature:

REVIEW 3

Lecturer's Comments	Student's Comments	Date:
		Action

Lecturer's Signature: Student's Signature:

On completion please forward original to Sue Thatcher, Copies to Lecturer & Tutor

112455.DOC

112455.DOC

Appendix 4·4

Bridgwater College: Additional support cost pro forma

Bridgwater College ADDITIONAL SUPPORT COST PRO FORMA 01-Nov-98	Name:			
	ID No:			
	Course:			
	Tutor:			
	Duration:	1 Year		
	FT/PT:	FT	Start Date:	07-Sep-98

	Cost Per Hour	Hrs Per Wk	Wks Per Year	Cost Per Year
PRE ENTRY				
School Liaison/Reveiws/Visits				£ -
Case Conference/Reviews				£ -
College Visits				£ -
				£ -
Other: (please state)				£ -
ON PROGRAMME				
Additional Assessment				£ -
Additional Teaching				£ -
Additional Teaching				£ -
Additional Tutoring				£ -
Communicator/Facilitator				£ -
Placement Co-ordinator				£ -
Technician				£ -
Technician				£ -
Learning Support Coordinator				£ -
Notetaker				£ -
Teaching Assistant				£ -
Classroom Assistant				£ -
Personal Care				£ -
Basic Skills Tuition				£ -
Instructor Support				£ -
Adjusted SSR				
Full Time Group Size:				£0.00
Part Time Group Size:				£0.00
Hrs Load Band:				
Other Professional Services				£ -
Exam Costs				£ -
Exam Exemptions				£ -
Admin costs				£ -
Reprographics				£ -
Materials				£ -
PROGRESSION				
Review Meetings/Liaison				£ -
Communication Networking				£ -
Other:				£ -

Additional Support Band	#N/A		Total Cost:	£ -
Additional Units	#N/A			
Income from Other Sources				
Staff Completing Costing (Initials)			Dated:	01-Nov-98

Students Signature:

Nov98.xls, Master

Raising achievement

Appendix 4·5

Bridgwater College: Request for permission to admit a student who does not meet entry criteria 1998/99

BRIDGWATER COLLEGE

REQUEST FOR PERMISSION TO ADMIT A STUDENT WHO DOES NOT MEET COURSE ENTRY CRITERIA 1998/99

Student's Name:

Student grades at entry:

Course Title:

Course entry criteria

Reasons for offering student a place

Steps to be taken to minimise drop-out (e.g. Additional Support)

Name of Tutor:

Date of Request:

COMMENTS AND DECISION

Head of Learner Services:

Date:

083982.frm

Appendix 5

Supplementary materials relating to processes for raising achievement

Appendix 5·1

Liverpool Community College: Retention checklist for managers 1999/2000

Liverpool COMMUNITY COLLEGE

Retention Checklist for Managers 99/2000

A great deal of research has been carried out into retention in FE colleges in recent years. The following have emerged as Key factors in retaining students:

* appropriate placement on courses
* student sociability
* teaching methods
* pastoral and student support functions.

The following list is by no means exhaustive but may help to ensure that we're working individually and collectively to improve retention.

		Comment

1.	Is the whole course team involved in
	
	    * setting retention targets?
	    * discussing collectively ways of improving retention?
	    * regularly monitoring retention levels using MIS info. as appropriate?	

2.	Are course descriptions in the ESP as full and accurate as possible?	

3.	Do pre-entry guidance practices ensure that students are appropriately recruited to courses in terms of
	
	    * qualifications/skills (using the college initial assessment tests where appropriate)?
	    * intended destinations?	

4.	Are induction plans
	
	    * in place?
	    * interesting and appropriate to the student group?	

5.	How will the learning support needs of students be identified in the interview/induction stage of the course?	
6.	Are course teams carrying out team-building activities with their students during the early weeks of the course?	

	Comment
7. Are weekly attendance checks taking place during the early part of the course?	
8. Are tutorials for courses of 450 hours * operating properly? (eg. students allocated a personal tutor as they are timetabled.) * is there a planned programme of relevant activities?	
9. Are termly reviews of progress in place for **every** student?	
10. Are the Curriculum Customer Support officers asked to follow up absenteeism where appropriate?	
11. Do course teams formally discuss student related matters? eg. * are efforts made to stagger assignment dates? * is student progress a standard agenda item at course team meetings?	
12. Does each member of the course team know what individual and collective responsibility s/he has in relation to retention? eg. * who takes responsibility for inducting late starters and ensuring that they settle in quickly? * who is responsible for organising tutorials for students following courses at several centres?	
13. Are students views regularly canvassed by each course team * through the student representative system? (obligatory for courses of 450 hours or more from 1998/9). * through course evaluation?	
14. Are there means whereby good practice in teaching and learning is shared across course teams? eg. * do staff team-teach? * is there peer observation of teaching and learning?	

Comment

15. Have you put in place plans to observe teaching and learning in your curriculum area?

16. Are parents/carers of students aged under 19 invited to open evenings, exhibitions etc. as appropriate?

17. Do course teams include retention strategies in their self assessment reports?

18. Are there ways in which HoFs could help course teams to work together? eg.

    *   by ensuring that staff are appropriately grouped together in staff workrooms.

Please note: the Calendar of Activities in the Course Team Manual covers most of the retention-related procedures and reviews.

Appendix 5·2

East Birmingham College: Checklist for tutors

Looking at Student Achievements - possible factors to consider

1) Are all of the students who achieved in your area enrolled in the college?

2) Do you have official copies (evidence) of the actual achievements in your area?

3) Have you discussed the achievements with staff / course team; **COMMENTS?**

4) Have all of your students been properly entered for their award(s) e.g. OCNWM **including second and third awards?**

5) Has all the paperwork been completed so that students can be awarded their qualification(s) (all such paperwork can be checked with Shirley);

6) Do you know who the moderators are for your area? Has moderation taken place?

7) Have you spoken with staff teaching in your area about their achievements?

8) Have the achievements for your area been handed in to the Student Achievement Unit?

9) Do staff in your area understand the difference between a full / part award / pass?

10) Can staff in your area compare their achievement figures with previous years / national average e.g. where are the copies of your previous years results?

11) What have you done as a result of this year's achievements? What plans have the staff / course teams made in light of their achievements?

12) Have you looked to see if there are any distinctive patterns of achievements in your area e.g. good / poor results, mode of attendance, day - evening etc?

13) Do staff in your area take responsibility for their achievements. If staff were asked to discuss and explain their achievements with an inspector, what would the result be?

Pass Rate:
Numbers of students entered for a qualification, against the numbers who gain the qualification. You can compare this figure with the national figures.

Achievement Rate:
Number of students who achieve their learning goal at the end of the programme, against the numbers who started the programme.